Interactive
FAMILY WORSHIP IDEAS
for kids

Bill **Kirstein**

Pacific Press®
Publishing Association

Nampa, Idaho | Oshawa, Ontario, Canada
www.pacificpress.com

Copyright © 2015 by Pacific Press® Publishing Association
Published in the United States of America
All rights reserved.

The author assumes full responsibility for the accuracy of all facts and quotations as cited in this book.

Texts credited to Clear Word are from *The Clear Word,* copyright © 1994, 2000, 2003, 2004, 2006 by Review and Herald® Publishing Association. All rights reserved.

Texts credited to NIV are from the *Holy Bible, New International Version.* Copyright © 1973, 1978, 1984, 2011 by Biblica, Inc. Used by permission. All rights reserved.

Texts credited to NKJV are from the New King James Version. Copyright © 1979, 1980, 1982 by Thomas Nelson, Inc. Used by permission. All rights reserved.

Bible texts credited to NRSV are from the New Revised Standard Version of the Bible, copyright © 1989 by the Division of Christian Education of the National Council of Churches of Christ in the U.S.A. Used by permission.

This book was
Edited by Gerald Wheeler
Copyedited by Judy Blodgett
Cover designed by Bryan Gray / Review and Herald® Design Center
Interior designed by Review and Herald® Design Center
Interior illustrations © Review and Herald® Publishing Association: pages 13, 14, 17, 18, 19, 21, 22, 23, 39, 44, 49, 55, 56, 58, 60, 89, 95, 103, 107
Unless otherwise noted, all photos are © Thinkstock.com
Typeset: Minion Pro 13/15

PRINTED IN THE U.S.A.

You can obtain additional copies of this book by calling toll-free 1-800-765-6955 or by visiting www.adventistbookcenter.com.

Library of Congress Cataloging-in-Publication Data
Kirstein, Bill.
 Interactive family worship ideas for kids / Bill Kirstein.
    pages cm
  ISBN 13: 978-0-8163-5778-9
  ISBN 10: 0-8163-5778-1
 1. Christian education—Home training. 2. Christian education of children. 3. Families—Religious life. 4. Seventh-day Adventists—Doctrines. I. Title.
  BV1590.K57 2014
  249.088'286732—dc23
                               2014009239

January 2015

A Note From the Author

Making the Sabbath a delight was one of the objectives that our family intentionally planned for each week. The fun began on Friday night. But sometime during the week I would visit a Christian bookstore and purchase inexpensive booklets, pencils, and various trinkets. Then I would wrap them up, bring them home, and place them in a worship bag for the boys to open at sundown. To them it was like Christmas every Friday night! The things didn't cost much, but by our making a big deal of the event it became a huge one to the boys, one for which they could hardly wait. Sometimes to heighten the fun, we would hide clues all over the house—under a chair, in a flowerpot, behind books, under their pillow, etc. Each clue would send them chasing to the next, until they found the desired "Friday night surprise" at the end of the hunt.

It was fun times like these that our now-grown boys still remember and have asked me to write down so that they can enjoy them again with their kids. Thus this book.

My hope is that through these games, stories, quizzes, and unique nature walks you and your family will also find an enjoyable approach to family worship, and that each of you will be drawn to your Creator through creative worship fun.

—Bill Kirstein

Contents

Sections:

Interactive Worships 9

Fascinating Quizzories 39

Purposeful Nature Walks 47

Quiet Worship Ideas 64

Meaningful Stories 79

Prayer and Praise Ideas 99

Interactive Worships

Here are a few worship activities and games that involve people of all sizes—the more the merrier!

1

Hunt. Show. Tell.
A wannabe scavenger hunt—indoors or out

Instructions: *Divide into two teams. Photocopy or cut out the lists below, then have the teams find the items and keep them on their plate. Substitute items as appropriate. Review the items, then ask the questions below. Judges determine the best answers. Make a new list and play again.*

TEAM A	TEAM B
soap	eraser
bread	flower
pinecone	string
paper clip	green stick
iPhone	Bible
leaf	salt
drinking glass	fruit
rock	coins
book	feather
lightbulb	CD
pencil	hat

Ask each team the following questions:

1. Which items on your list will be found in heaven?

2. Which items will not be needed in heaven? Why?

3. What might we use instead of these things?

4. Share an object lesson from two items on your list.

10   Interactive Family Worship Ideas for Kids

Guess-It Bag

Instructions: *Before worship begins, place five* containers, such as a paper bag, small box, designer bag, wrapped jar, boot/shoe, etc., on the table. Number each on the outside but have the number upside down. Each will contain one human-made item, such as a key, paper clip, spoon, pencil, fishing line, etc.*

How to Play:

Each player is to choose one container, but will take his or her turn in play by the number on the container. No one is to see the item except the one holding the container.

The player looks inside and tries to describe the item while the others attempt to guess what it is by the verbal description only. If no one can guess within two minutes, the bag gets passed to the next person to play.

All the things in the containers are human-made. When the item is guessed, the one holding the container shows it and explains how it is similar in design or function to something in nature, or to something Jesus might have used while here on earth.

---

*Varies with number of players.

Interactive Worships   11

Clothesline Baseball Worship

Theme: Garden of Eden. Most of the questions come from *The Bible Story*, volume 1, pages 53 and 57.

Instructions: *Photocopy and fold the questions below and then hang them along a line that stretches across the room. The kids will select a question from the line, read it aloud, then answer the question. If they answer correctly (according to the "umpire"), they advance to the base shown on the question. But if they cannot answer, they are out. They must wait their turn to draw again. When a kid gets on base, he or she stays there until their next turn or until someone knocks them to another base or home plate. Whenever they cross the "plate" they get the points shown in parentheses. Don't let the game become competitive.*

What was called God's "fairest" creation? (*one free point*)

What did God use to "build" a woman? (*one free point*)

Where did God put Adam and Eve after He created them? (*one free point*)

When God planted the Garden of Eden, did He use seeds? (*double*)

Did God make Adam and Eve a palace home of gold and silver? (*single*)

How did God's huge garden keep watered? (*single*)

What was God's original system of surround-sound music? (*double*)

What did God place in the center of the garden? (*triple*)

Why did God place a fruit tree in the garden from which Adam and Eve could not eat? (*home run*)

Why did God create nighttime in the garden? (*triple*)

Why did God create a rest day when no one was tired? (*home run*)

What do you think God did with Adam and Eve on the first Sabbath? (*triple*)

Of all the things that God made that first week, what was His "prize" creation? (*single*)

Why didn't Adam and Eve need a shelter over their heads? (*double*)

What did God do with the tree of life? (*home run*)

Interactive Family Worship Ideas for Kids

What on Earth Will Heaven Be Like?

Instructions: *Tag three areas on the floor at some distance apart with masking tape and label them "True," "False," and "Not Sure." Explain that the players are to run to the box that shows their answer. If they don't know the answer, stand in the "Not Sure" box, then discuss the question.*

This quiz also makes a great children's story for church, but use hand gestures instead of running.

Heaven

1. T/F All the flowers in heaven will be pure white.
2. T/F More people live on earth today than there are angels in heaven.
3. T/F Someday the earth will burn up completely and be remade.
4. T/F We will need angel police to keep Satan and His evil angels out of heaven.
5. T/F Heaven will have many kinds of animals, birds, flowers, and fruit that we have not yet seen, smelled, or tasted.
6. T/F Jesus has not had any water since He drank it with His disciples while here on earth.
7. T/F When we see Jesus for the first time, He will have scars on *both* hands.
8. T/F No human has ever gone to or seen heaven before.
9. T/F It will *not* be necessary for us to build our homes in heaven since Jesus will have already built *everything* for us.
10. T/F Someday heaven will be relocated.
11. T/F Heaven will have *no* musical instruments, only choirs.
12. T/F We will travel to other solar systems from heaven.
13. T/F *Only* humans just like us dwell on the other planets.
14. T/F Our angel will tell us *only* the unsafe things we've done.
15. T/F In heaven we will be able to talk with God the Father.

Interactive Worships

Scriptoleous Guessing Quiz

Instructions: *Read aloud and challenge one or a team.*

1. There were **three** men in the fiery furnace. Name them. *(Shadrach, Meshach, Abednego)* (Daniel 3:23)
2. T/F The serpent in the Garden of Eden was multicolored. *(true)*
3. God told Moses how to build the earthly sanctuary. What kind of wood was he to use for the ark of the covenant? *(shittim or acacia)* (Exodus 25:10)
4. How many lions were in the lions' den: 3, 7, 10? *(not told)*
5. What is the name of the man who baptized Jesus? *(John)* (Matthew 3:13)
6. Name the first four books of the New Testament. *(Matthew, Mark, Luke, John)*
7. In Jesus' parable, what did a woman find in her house that caused her to celebrate? *(coin)* (Luke 15:9)
8. What was Jesus' earthly father's name? *(Joseph)* (Matthew 2:13)
9. What was created on the sixth day? *(man and animals)* (Genesis 1:24-31)
10. a. How much of our money belongs to God? *(all)*
    b. How much does He ask us to faithfully return to Him? *(one tenth)* (Malachi 3:10)
11. Name Noah's three sons that went into the ark. *(Shem, Ham, Japheth)* (Genesis 6:10, 18)
12. What was the name of the man Jesus raised from the dead? *(Lazarus)* (John 11:14, 43, 44)
13. What was Jesus' cousin's name? *(John)* (Matthew 3:13; Luke 1:36-80)
14. What very unusual thing did Moses find while walking through the desert? *(burning bush)* (Exodus 3:2)
15. Name four of Jesus' disciples. *(Simon Peter, Andrew, James, John, Philip, Bartholomew, Thomas, Matthew, James, Thaddaeus, Simon, Judas)* (Matthew 10:2-4)

Silent Scavenger Hunt

Instructions: *Enjoy a Bible scavenger hunt. Gather together such items as a basket, old coin, old pottery, a bag of seeds, faded cloth or burlap, small jars, replicas of Roman helmet or sword, straw—anything the people of Bible times might have used. Hide them when the kids aren't looking—around the room or yard before church. After lunch, announce the game and the items you've hidden, and let them go! They are to **find, but not touch**, as many as they can in three minutes, then take you around and show where each is hidden. The anticipation will be as fun as the hunt! They can now rehide them for each other. Discuss one or several of the items in worship. Don't let it become competitive.*

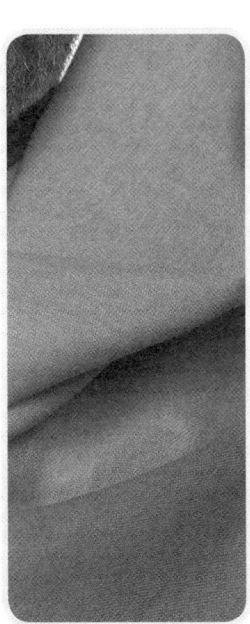

Interactive Worships 15

Jerusalem *Times*
Interview 1

Instructions: *Here are eight Bible character interviews for your kids to role-play. The interviews allow them to think about the Bible character. Recording the interviews will add even more meaning, and your kids will love to listen to them later.*

Dress the kids in Bible-type costumes (bathrobes, bandanna on head, bare feet or sandals, etc.) and have them answer the questions as if they were the actual person in the Bible story. The moderator is the local newspaper reporter interviewing them about their experience.

Jonah

Thank you, Jonah, for taking a minute to answer a few questions for our local paper. I'm sure your story will be of great interest to our readers.

- Where were you going on this commercial sailing vessel? Why?
- What happened that caused you to get thrown overboard?
- Do you know how to swim? Did you hang on to anything from the boat?
- What's this about being swallowed by a big fish? Is that true?
- What was it like inside the stomach of a fish? Did it stink in there? Was it dark?
- Do you think God saw you in there and kept you alive? How did you breathe?
- Did your skin burn from the digestive juices in the stomach of the fish?
- How did you get out? How did you get that fishy smell off yourself?
- Where did you go? How did you know where you were? Did anyone believe your story?
- Did you ever see anyone from the sailing ship again? What might they have asked you about your experience?
- Did you ever tell any little kids about your amazing trip to the bottom of the ocean?
- What else can you tell us about this strange ordeal?

Thank you, Jonah. This will appear in Tuesday's Jerusalem *Times* newspaper.

Jerusalem *Times*
Interview 2

Daniel

Good morning! I'm a reporter with the Jerusalem *Times* newspaper. Daniel, thank you for answering a few questions for next Thursday's issue.

- First of all, is your story about spending the night in the king's den of lions true?

- Why did they throw you into the lions' den? Why didn't the king change the rules for you?

- Why didn't you just stop praying for a few days or just shut your windows?

- How many men threw you into the den? Were you scared? Were they scared?

- Were the lions noisy at night? Were they hungry? How many were in there?

- Did you break any bones when you hit the bottom of the lions' den?

- Did it stink in there? Was it dark? Could you hear the guards outside talking?

- Did you see bones on the floor? Was there any light during the night?

- Did the lions attack you? What did you do to fight them off?

- Did you feel that God had forsaken you? Did you see any angels in there?

- How did you get out? What happened to the guards?

- Would you like to tell us anything else that you thought about at the time or since then?

Interactive Worships

Jerusalem *Times*
Interview 3

Adam

Good morning, Adam! I'm with the Jerusalem *Times* newspaper and would like to ask you a few questions. Do you have time? Thank you.

- What is the first thing you remember? Was God there?
- What did the world look like around you? Was it flat or hilly?
- What did you think of all those animals? Were you afraid of any of them?
- About how big were the elephants in the Garden of Eden? Where there any snakes there?
- What was the most beautiful bird you remember seeing? What color was it?
- Did all the flowers smell good? Which one did you like best? What color was it?
- What was your favorite food? Did you pick it off a tree or pull it out of the ground?
- Do you remember God putting you to sleep? Was there a scar in your side after God took out one of your ribs? Did it hurt? Could you feel the rib missing?
- What did you think when you saw Eve? Was she beautiful? What color was her hair?
- What did God tell you about Eve? What did God tell Eve about you?
- Where was your favorite place to go in the garden with Eve? Was it near the water?
- Did you swim? Were there waterfalls? lakes? rivers?
- Would you like to see the Garden of Eden again?

Thank you, Adam. Your story is truly amazing.

Jerusalem *Times*
Interview 4

Eve

Good morning, Eve! I'm with the Jerusalem *Times* newspaper and would like to ask you a few questions. Would you allow me to do so?

- The Bible tells us that you were made by the hand of God Himself. Do you feel special?
- What was the first thing you saw when you opened your eyes for the first time?
- Did you ever see yourself—like in a reflection of your face in the water?
- Did you think Adam was handsome? How long was his hair? What color were his eyes?
- When God introduced you to Adam, did He give you any instructions?
- What was your favorite animal in the garden? Did you wear a flower in your hair?
- Did you have any pets? What was your favorite fruit? What was Adam's favorite fruit?
- One day you left Adam's side. Why? Where did you go? What did you find?
- What color was the fruit on the tree of the knowledge of good and evil? Was it poisonous?
- Why did you want to eat the fruit? Who told you it was OK to eat?
- Were there snakes in the garden? What color was the serpent in the tree?
- Did the fruit you ate from that tree taste good? How did you feel when you bit into it?
- What did you say to Adam? What did Adam say to you? What did you say to God?
- What made you feel worse—eating the forbidden fruit or disappointing God? Why?
- If you could live that moment over again, what would you do different?
- What will you like to see the most when you see the Garden of Eden again?

Interactive Worships

Jerusalem *Times*
Interview 5

Mary

Mary, I'm with the Jerusalem *Times* newspaper, and we've been asked to write a report on your amazing life. Can you spare a couple minutes?

- You must have been very special to be chosen to carry Jesus. Were you afraid?
- Were your friends happy for you? Were you happy? was Joseph?
- Did you want to ask God any questions? What were some of them?
- Were you afraid to travel so many miles on a donkey's back? Were you comfortable?
- When Joseph had to find a place to spend the night, how many inns did he try?
- What did you think when Joseph found a cattle stall to stay in? Was that OK?
- Was it dirty? Did it smell bad? Did you have food? water? Did you have clean straw?
- What kinds of animals were there with you? Were the animals quiet?
- When Baby Jesus was born, what did you use to clean Him up?
- Was He a pretty baby? Did Joseph hold Him? Did the innkeeper come out to see Him?
- What did the Wise Men say about Him? How long did they stay?
- When the shepherds arrived, what did they do with their sheep? Were they excited?
- What did the shepherds say about the baby? Did they bring any gifts for Him?
- When Jesus was 10 years old, did the neighbor kids like Him? Were they nice to Him?
- How did you feel to see your Son, Jesus, die on a cross? Did you talk to Him there?
- When you see Jesus again, what will you ask Him?

Thank you, Mary. I plan to be in heaven with some questions for Him too!

20 Interactive Family Worship Ideas for Kids

Jerusalem *Times*
Interview 6

Joseph

Mr. Joseph, sir, I'm with the Jerusalem *Times* newspaper, and we want to write a short story about a part of your life. Do you have a minute?

- Joseph, you were planning to marry a young girl in your town by the name of Mary. Were you excited when she told you she was going to have a baby?
- How could you afford to take care of both Mary *and* a new baby? What did you do?
- Is it true that an angel talked with you in a dream about marrying this girl?
- Are you sure this was a dream from God, or did you just eat a big supper?
- When you found out the baby was to be the Messiah, what did you think? Were you happy?
- The angel told you to name Him "Jesus." Did you like that name? Did Mary?
- Did you tell anyone what was happening? What did your mother and father say? What did the neighbors say?
- So you and Mary got married, and shortly after that, you got a notice that you and she had to go to Bethlehem to register and pay taxes. Were you afraid to travel with her like that?
- What was the name of your donkey? Was it gentle to ride? Did it carry supplies, too?
- When you got to Bethlehem, were there lots of people? Were they nice to you?
- When the innkeepers saw that your wife was soon to have a baby, were they nicer to you?
- How much did you pay for a dirty stall in a manger? Were you happy? comfortable?
- Are you glad you had a part in raising the most important Child ever born?
- What will you say to Him when you meet again in heaven?

Interactive Worships

Jerusalem *Times*
Interview 7

Moses

Good morning, Mr. Moses! I'm with the Jerusalem *Times* newspaper, and we're interviewing biblical celebrities such as you. Might we take a minute or so of your time to ask a few personal questions?

- I heard that as a baby you were put in a basket and placed in the river. True? Why?
- Wasn't the river an unsafe place for a baby? Did anyone watch over you?
- How did you get from the river to the royal palace? Were you educated in Egyptian customs?
- After you spent your younger years in the palace, you suddenly left. Why?
- Where did you go and what did you do? Why did you go back to Egypt?
- Did you volunteer to go to ask Pharaoh to let the Israelites leave Egypt?
- Did you go alone? Were you afraid?
- What did you say or do to convince Pharaoh to let the Israelites leave? Did it work?
- What were some of the plagues that struck Egypt? Did they bother you?
- So Pharaoh released Israel from Egyptian bondage. Where did you go and what did you eat?
- Do you feel that God was looking after you and the entire camp of Israel?
- Oh, there's so much more I'd like to ask, but one last question: Throughout your long lifetime, do you feel God took special care of you, and does He still care for His people?

Interactive Family Worship Ideas for Kids

Jerusalem *Times*
Interview 8

Paul

Mr. Paul, sir, I'm with the Jerusalem *Times,* and I've been asked to write a report about your recent shipwreck. May I ask a few questions?

- I understand that your ship sailing to Italy stopped at Fair Havens and spent too much time there, and when it was time to depart you recommended against it. Is that true?
- Were you concerned about sailing in the winter storms during October? Why?
- Did the captain take your advice, or did he listen to the owner of the ship?
- What happened?
- Did the sailors like the idea? Were they scared of the heavy winds?
- Were you blown way off course? Did the ship have a lifeboat?
- What did the crew do to save the ship?
- Did anyone get seasick? Did you have food?
- What did you do?
- How did you know no one would die?
- Did any sailors try to escape? Did anyone escape?
- Did you encourage the men to eat something? Did they? Did you pray?
- Do you remember how many men were on board?
- Where did the boat finally end up?
- What did the captain want the men to do?
- What about those who couldn't swim?
- Do you believe God saved you and the crew?

  Thank you, sir, for your time.

(Read the story in Acts 27:1-44.)

Interactive Worships 23

Situation Hot Seat

Instructions: *Put your kids in a "hot seat" and watch them squirm for answers to these dilemmas. You'll be surprised at how sharp they are!*

1. **Joan's family** moved into a new neighborhood next to a family who had two girls her same age. Sabbath morning the neighbor girls storm out of their house dressed nicely but arguing heatedly. They are both very angry. Glancing over the fence, they see you noticing them and immediately quiet down. Shortly their mother comes out, and they speed off in the car. Later your family leaves for church. Upon arriving at the church, you find that the girls are the greeters at the door. Embarrassed, they fake a smile. Even though you are the guest at their church, what do you say to them?

2. **Bill's parents** have gone to the grocery store and leave him home alone. He turns on the TV and cranks up the volume to a program called *Slimeball Sam*. But at the most dramatic moment of the show, the doorbell rings, and he runs to find . . . the pastor standing there. He's come to see Bill's parents! You are Bill. What do you say?

3. **You don't like Johnny,** the new fat boy in your school, so you spread the rumor that his dad is a criminal in the county jail—even though you know he's really a doctor. One day you're walking home from school when Johnny and his father pull up and offer you a ride home. You accept. As you are riding along, Johnny's dad asks if you know how the rumor about him being in jail got started. What do you say to him?

4. **You see someone** put sand in the lunch of a boy at school who never eats in the school cafeteria with you or your friends. Other kids tell you he's just being a snob, but in fact he's very poor and can't afford the meals. What do you do when you learn the truth? What should the teacher do? What would Jesus do?

5. **Jesus comes** as a visitor to your Sabbath school. No one knows who He is. You arrive late, and your "friends" start teasing you. You're embarrassed. Does Jesus say anything to you or to the teasing boys? If so, what?

6. **Seven boys** get together for a pickup game of ball on the empty lot next to your house. It's late Friday afternoon. You know the game will not end until after sundown. The guys urge you to play to make the sides even. Do you play ball? How do you explain the situation to them?

7. **Your little brother** loves to come into your room when you're not around and to pull stuff out and play with it. He spills bottles, messes up your bed, and leaves everything a total disaster. How would Jesus handle this? How do you handle it?

8. **You hit someone** at school during recess because you believe they were

24   Interactive Family Worship Ideas for Kids

Situation Hot Seat

playing unfairly. When the teacher asks about it, you lie and say you didn't hit anyone! But the first-grade teacher saw the whole thing and tells your teacher the truth. What do you say when you're caught? How should your teacher handle this?

9. You and a friend are in Walmart just snooping around, waiting to go home. Your friend sees a wallet he likes and stuffs it into his pocket. You tell him he should put it back, but he refuses, runs, and disappears. As you leave the store an armed guard grabs *you* and says he saw *you* steal a wallet! How do you prove your innocence, yet keep your friendship intact?

10. You are with friends at Pizza Hut. You hear the teenage boy in the booth next to you telling his friends to watch CNN Tuesday night because CNN will be airing the Messiah's second coming live. He says the whole world will be watching on national television. You stand up and say to him: "_____."

11. Your neighbor girl comes to Sabbath school, at your invitation, for the first time. She's never been inside any church, so is very nervous. Your friends shun her because she is overweight, dressed in jeans, and wearing heavy makeup. What do you say to her? What do you say to them?

12. A neighbor kid invites you to his birthday party and tells you that his mother is fixing his favorite dish: roast pork sandwiches and grilled catfish. Do you go to the party? What do you say about the food?

13. You're walking home from school when a stranger walks up and offers you something that he promises will make you feel real good! How do you deal with this? What do you say?

14. You're in the grocery store and see a sign that reads: Bananas 5 for $1.00, 3 for $.75. You watch as an adult, whom you do not know, walks up and switches parts of the signs and takes five bananas for $.75 and goes to the counter. Do you tell the manager? the cashier? Do you correct the stranger and return the signs, or let it go?

15. You watch as an eighth grader from your school sneaks an umbrella from the rack and runs out the door. You believe it belongs to the principal, so you tell him about it. He doesn't believe the boy would do such a thing, but thanks you anyway. Later you overhear this same boy telling the principal that he believes someone in *your* classroom stole the umbrella. What do you say when you and your best friend are accused?

16. You invite a friend over after church to enjoy a meal with your family. After lunch the two of you take a nature walk, at which time he tells you he doesn't believe God exists. What do you say to him? What do you say to your parents?

17. Your best friend's grandmother dies. You go to the funeral. The next week in school she tells you she believes her grandmother is in heaven watching everything she does. What do you say to her? What Bible text could you share about death?

Interactive Worships

Secret Orders

Instructions: *Kids love to keep secrets, and this might be just the spice you need to kick up your family worship. I used these in Sabbath school and asked the kids to keep their assignment secret all week just to make it more suspenseful. Use them as a worship "extra" and, just for fun, let the kids save their secret until Friday evening worship. Here are some of those "secret" assignments:*

1. Bring in an arrangement of fresh-picked flowers next week.
2. Play a favorite CD for worship and tell why it's your favorite.
3. Help someone, other than family, and tell about it in worship next week.
4. Write a poem and read it to the family and with us next week.
5. Draw a picture and share it at worship next week.
6. Find a "nature's face" in wood or stone, and share it with everyone next week.
7. Find an old bird nest and show it to us next week.
8. Make up a Bible quiz for the family.
9. Tell why you like being an Adventist.
10. Tell about something that interests you a lot. Show an example next week.
11. Bring in several newspaper clippings that support why you believe Jesus is coming soon.
12. Bring examples of things that make music, some created by God and others by human beings.
13. Bring something sticky and share an object lesson about it.
14. Bring in something very small. Tell us about it.
15. Mark on the wall Adam's, Goliath's, and your height.
16. Bring in something that smells good and share an object lesson from it.

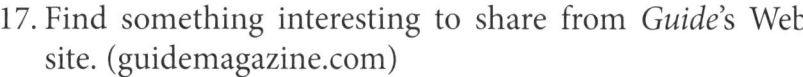

17. Find something interesting to share from *Guide*'s Web site. (guidemagazine.com)

18. Do something nice for an older person and tell us about it.

19. Find and show us something alive that looks funny and makes you smile.

20. Tell a short story about your pet that your family hasn't heard.

21. Find and read a verse in the Bible that you especially like.

22. Make a miniature model of something that Jesus might have used in the carpenter's shop. Show us.

23. Make a bouquet of fall leaves or summer flowers for the table. Show us.

24. Make a calendar or poster that shows what you did each day of the past week.

25. Draw a diagram of the Jewish tabernacle indicating where some of the furniture was located. Show us.

Interactive Worships

Brown Bag Worship

This is one of the most creative yet simple worship activities we've enjoyed. Even Gram and Gramps will get into this one.

Instructions: *Place in a large paper bag various objects from around the house, such as a nail, watch, block of wood, soap, magnet, etc. (enough objects for all the players). Pass the bag around and everyone draws out one item. No one is to look inside the bag. When all have taken an object, the first person shows and tells the group what he or she has, and what Bible story or object lesson they might draw from it. When the speaker is finished, anyone else may add their thoughts. It's amazing how many lessons you can draw from simple, everyday things.*
Close with a short scripture and prayer.

Guess This Tune

Instructions: *Let someone play just a measure or two of some familiar hymn, then abruptly stop, and have someone guess the name of the song. If they guess it correctly, they get to whisper to the instrumentalist the next selection for everyone to guess. Repeat as long as you wish to play.*

Create a Second Coming Banner

Instructions: *Spread out a large sheet of paper or cloth on the table or floor, add some markers or crayons and scissors, and let the family create a banner using one or combining several of these elements:* **flames, trumpets, crowns, clouds, stars, lightning.**
Add to these subjects and/or make up other design elements. Let each individual explain his or her choices and why they look forward to Jesus' return.

A Worship of Praise

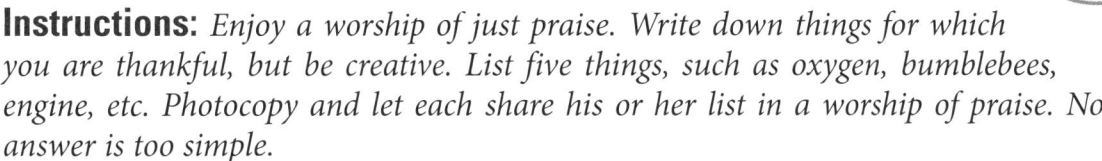

Instructions: *Enjoy a worship of just praise. Write down things for which you are thankful, but be creative. List five things, such as oxygen, bumblebees, engine, etc. Photocopy and let each share his or her list in a worship of praise. No answer is too simple.*

"Lord, I am thankful for many things, but I must mention here a few things I seldom think of . . .

1. _____
2. _____
3. _____
4. _____
5. _____

Close by reading Psalm 150 together and singing "Praise God From Whom All Blessings Flow," *The Seventh-day Adventist Hymnal,* nos. 694, 695.

"Chairicho" Is Goin' Down

Instructions: *Set several small wooden chairs in the middle of the room and tie a thread to the top of them. Make some "homemade" instruments and march around "Jericho" six times—with the "ark" leading the way. On the seventh time around, celebrate with shouting and blowing of the instruments and let an adult ceremoniously pull the chairs over (don't hit any kids!) and watch all the "walls'" come tumbling down. Read the story in Joshua 6:1-20 from* The Clear Word *or* The Bible Story, *volume 3, pages 88-91.*

Interactive Worships 29

The Beatitude Attitude

Instructions: Read Matthew 5:3-12, NIV.

Idea 1: Copy the beatitudes, and attach the ones from the first half on the backs of half of the players, and the second half on the rest. Let everyone try to match up, till all the beatitudes are complete. Then say them in order.

Idea 2: Same as above, but let one person come to the center of the room. Someone reads his or her beatitude, and the person with the second half of the beatitude joins him or her in the center.

First Half of the Beatitude

"Blessed are the poor in spirit,
"Blessed are those who mourn,
"Blessed are the meek,
"Blessed are those who hunger and thirst for righteousness,
"Blessed are the merciful,
"Blessed are the pure in heart,
"Blessed are the peacemakers,
"Blessed are those who are persecuted because of righteousness,
"Blessed are you when people insult you . . . and falsely say all kinds of evil against you because of me.

Second Half of the Beatitude

for theirs is the kingdom of heaven."
for they will be comforted."
for they will inherit the earth."
for they will be filled."
for they will be shown mercy."
for they will see God."
for they will be called the children of God."
for theirs is the kingdom of heaven."
Rejoice and be glad, because great is your reward in heaven."

30   Interactive Family Worship Ideas for Kids

The Beatitudes Applied

Instructions: *Read the stories below and decide which beatitude works.*

A little girl is very upset and crying. A young boy notices her tears and asks about her problem. She says her kitten died. He tells her his mother cat just had kittens and promises to bring her one. When he does, she's thrilled! What beatitude fits? *(They that mourn.)*

Your neighbor family is Jewish. One day they tell you they want to know about Jesus. Your family has them over and tells them about Jesus and more. What beatitude fits? *(Hunger and thirst for righteousness.)*

Two boys are fighting on the playground at school. A young girl comes up to them and tells them to stop and talk through their differences. They do. What beatitude fits? *(Blessed are the peacemakers.)*

When the teacher calls the class in from recess, you make your way to the drinking fountain before returning to the classroom. Immediately three boys jump in line ahead of you at the fountain and you politely let them get drinks first. What beatitude fits? *(Blessed are the poor in spirit.)*

An old woman lives down the hill from you and quietly shares from her simple life for the needs of others. She gives eggs to the hungry and blankets to the homeless, and faithfully writes letters of encouragement to prisoners. Never asking for recognition, she is a quiet witness to many. What beatitude fits? *(Blessed are the meek.)*

At the end of a very busy day, an exhausted doctor visits his young patient one last time, putting a cold cloth on her head and giving her an extra blanket to keep her warm. What beatitude fits? *(Blessed are the merciful.)*

Some neighbor kids have gathered under a streetlight on your corner, telling nasty jokes and laughing. You happen to walk up and hear them, and, instead of joining them, you quietly excuse yourself and go home. What beatitude fits? *(Blessed are the pure in heart.)*

The authorities tell a young boy that he must go to school on Sabbath or be punished and put in prison. He doesn't show up for school on Sabbath morning. The police arrest and imprison him without food for one week. What beatitude fits? *(Blessed are the persecuted.)*

The neighbor boys called Susan a fool because she wouldn't take God's name in vain, as they did. They threw rocks at her and hit her for believing that God was alive and saw all the things they did. What beatitude fits? *(Blessed are you when people insult you.)*

Interactive Worships

The Journey of a Blind Man

Mark 10:46-52: Jesus heals a blind beggar.

Blindfold a child and tell him or her that you are going to lead them, but only with words, to the "master" who can "heal" them of their "blindness."

Have the family sit in somewhat of a circle and appoint three volunteers—one to be the blind man, a director, and the master. Blindfold the one person, and place several harmless obstacles that he or she must not touch in the circle. Tell the blindfolded child that they will be directed to the master **by words only.** If they stumble against any of the obstacles, they are out of the game. They must listen and respond very carefully. When he or she reaches the master across the room, he removes the blindfold, and the child can "see" again. All celebrate the healing!

If there are several children, others will undoubtedly want to give it a try. Rearrange the obstacles, blindfold another volunteer, appoint another master and director, and watch the kids work together.

To close, remind kids that Jesus is the only true Master, and that He alone can restore sight to a blind person. Read Psalm 146:5-8 and end with a prayer of gratitude for the gift of sight.

Worship Time

Instructions: *Give each family member a question to answer.*

I think daily worship for kids my age is important because . . .

Share something you've learned in your personal worship.

I prefer: Family worship? Private worship? Because?

I think we should have family worship on Sabbath, because . . .

I would like to have Jesus come to our family worship and . . .

Name three things that could interfere with family worship.

Describe an unusual worship you've seen or taken part in.

If I were asked to have family worship, I would . . .

Name three things I think worship should include.

I think the best time for family worship is . . .

ToolSpeak

Introduction: *Place a number of hand tools on the table and let each player select one. Then answer the following questions:*

1. How could a junior-age boy or girl help someone with this tool?

2. If this tool were a person, how valuable could it be to Jesus' kingdom?

3. If you were this tool, would you tell your owner how best to use you?

4. What spiritual lesson can you draw from this tool?

Interactive Worships

Seek It, See It, 'n' Say It

20

Instructions: *Let the kids find the items shown below, then spread them out and carefully read the verse with each one. Now cover them with a paper cup and thoroughly mix the cups. Let each player uncover one cup and say the appropriate verse. If they cannot repeat the verse from its clue, read the verse below each item. If still unable, they lose a turn. Go to the next player. Remember to rescramble the cups. The objects act as visual reminders for learning the verse.*

(Note: If you cannot find any of these items in your area, substitute others as appropriate.)

STONE—"I will take out their stubborn hearts of stone" (Ezekiel 11:19, Clear Word).

Lifeless. Unfeeling. Cold—like the heart of a sinner. A stone cannot change itself.

LEAF—"The leaves of the tree are for the healing of the nations" (Revelation 22:2, NIV).

The leaves from the tree of life will heal people of all their diseases and sorrows.

WOOD—"That person is like a tree planted by streams of water" (Psalm 1:3).

The one who follows God's ways will be happy like a tree that grows beside water.

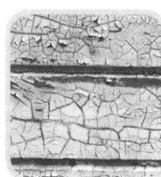

ACORN—"Thy word have I hid in mine heart" (Psalm 119:11).

Just as there is the promise of a tree in the heart of the acorn, so there is the promise of eternal life in the heart of one who keeps God's Word.

THORN—"The soldiers twisted a crown of thorns and put it on His head" (John 19:2, NKJV).

A painful crown of thorns could not keep Jesus from fulfilling His mission of love.

SEED POD—"God gave us the seed . . . and He's the One who made it grow" (1 Corinthians 3:6, Clear Word).

Filled with promise for another generation of life.

BERRY(IES)—"In the beginning He made everything beautiful" (Ecclesiastes 3:11, Clear Word).

Like jewels in the garden to give it added beauty.

34 Interactive Family Worship Ideas for Kids

Follow the Clues or Lose!

Instructions: *This game makes a great start to your worship. It is addicting to kids, and the suspense drives them on! They'll want to play it every week. Make sure that the youngest one(s) take part and that the older ones don't run ahead and ruin the fun for them.*

Place a teacup on the counter and tell kids to follow the instructions inside the cup. It might say: "Look in the windowsill for your next clue." That clue takes them to another clue. The game sends them all over the house searching for clues. "Look under your pillow, under the throw rug in the bathroom, the silverware drawer, the refrigerator door, etc." The more clues the better! Finally look in the oven (or wherever) where you'll find cookies (or whatever). That's optional—you could end with a package or inexpensive gift.

LESSON: Some people look in many places to find peace and happiness—things such as drugs, sports, movies, love, etc.—not realizing that what they're really searching for is Jesus. Once they find Him, they know that only He can bring true happiness and peace.

This is also fun to play outside, but in either case it takes some careful preplanning.

Interactive Worships

Our Family Reunion Worships

Instructions: *Each day of our family reunion was packed with fun, and it started with our morning worships. We prenumbered six small paper bags (that's how many days the family was together). Each bag contained a group activity and a story, both selected to be of interest to the youngest members. After breakfast we chose an adult to take the lead. We'd begin with a group song, try the activity, read the story, and close with prayer. Short but appropriate.*

DAY 1

Activity: See if you can fold a single piece of 8½" x 11" paper in half more than eight times. If you succeed, you'll be the first one ever to do it! *(It can't be done!)*

Story: Salina wanted to learn to play the saxophone. Well, really, her father wanted her to learn to play the saxophone, because he had learned to play when he was her age. So he showed her how to attach the curved neck piece to the main body, how to put the reed on the mouthpiece, slip the strap over her head, hook the strap to the saxophone, etc. All that was pretty easy. But then she tried to play—well, blow on the mouthpiece. Nothing happened. She tried again, but only a silly squeaky noise came out! When her father told her to blow harder, she did, and suddenly a terrifying loud blast of noise came blurting out of nowhere. It sounded like a bullfrog with laryngitis—only louder and not as pretty! It was definitely not musical!

"This thing is impossible to play!" she said. "It can't be done!" Her kind father suggested that perhaps the reed was too loose, or not straight, or . . . well, he tried, and it played beautifully. Eventually she did learn to play as well as her father, but not until after a lot more terrible sounds and a lot more practice.

Have you ever tried to do something that looked easy, but found that it was harder than you thought? Part of being really good at something is to make it look easy, as if anyone could do it. Some things can be deceptive.

Satan is a master at deceiving us. He's lied so long that he can make something look easy and guilt-free. But it's neither. There's always a consequence to everything we do and say. Sometimes it's for good, but if Satan is in it, it's for no good. Let's determine today that all of our efforts will be only for good. God can make music of lives that it would seem impossible to get even one note out of. But if God is in it—*it can be done, beautifully!*

Close with prayer.

DAY 2

Quick Quiz:

- The world's most popular fruit is _____. *(tomato)*

- A fresh egg will _____, but a stale one won't. *(sink in water)*
- Approximately three jars of _____ are sold every second. *(peanut butter)*
- More than 5 million _____ are made for kids every year. *(crayons)*

Story: Have you ever thought what the world would be like without color? if all the crayons in your box were gray? It would be very boring without bright-red tomatoes, blue skies, or colorful sunsets. Color is a special gift from God that makes our world a happier place.

Once a little girl began to worry because her mother had become very sick. What would she do if her mother didn't get well? When a nurse came to see her mother, the little girl slipped from her mother's bed to the windowsill. There she saw a perfect rainbow arching across the sky and remembered that God had made the rainbow. *It's His promise to everyone,* she thought. *If He can make the colors exactly the same in all the rainbows in the world, He can heal my mother—that's His promise, and I accept His promises by faith.* And with that thought the little girl felt better. And in a very short time, so did her mother!

The rainbow is our reminder that God will never flood the entire world again. What a colorful way to say, *I love you. You can trust Me for everything!*

Close with prayer.

DAY 3:

Activity: Squeeze your hands and fingers together tightly for five seconds. With hands still folded, lift your two index fingers straight up and far apart. They will draw together like magic!

Story: Did you ever want something really bad, ask your parents for it, and still not get it? Sometimes that happens, for all kinds of reasons. Well, God is more dependable than our parents, though He doesn't always give us everything we ask for. He loves us too much for that. Sometimes the things we ask for are not for our best good. But He always answers our prayers for our best good. Sometimes it's yes. Sometimes no. And sometimes wait. That's the hard one.

Once a little boy wanted a horse. His friend had a horse, and he wanted one too. In fact he wanted a horse more than anything he could think of. So he asked his dad to get him a horse. But his dad didn't give him a horse. Over time he got his son a cat, a dog, two guinea pigs, and some ducks, but not a horse. Did his dad not love him? Did he not hear his request? Why couldn't he have a horse?

Then his dad reminded him that there was just no space on their property for a big horse. The horse wouldn't be able to live on the little bit of grass in their backyard—and so who would feed the animal? Dad couldn't afford hay, and besides, the neighbors lived close, and the horse would begin to stink and could offend them. All good reasons *not* to get a horse. Reasons the little boy hadn't even thought of.

Even better than the boy's dad, God thinks of everything. Because He sees all sides of our prayer requests, He can always give us exactly what is for our best good in the end.

Close with prayer.

DAY 4:

Activity: Find a stick or pencil and let someone begin telling an imaginary story to it. After a sentence or two, pass the stick to another person who is to continue the story. No one can refuse.

Story: Johnny's dad loved to take him and his little sister out early in the morning to look for deer tracks they'd sometimes find along a dirt country road. They were always excited to find where a deer had crossed the road during the night. If they found tracks, they knew there might be deer still in the area. Better than seeing deer tracks was to spot the real thing, and to do that would really make their morning!

Some mornings the three would come home with big smiles, chattering with excitement. Without knowing it, they were leaving smile prints! Before their mother ever heard a word she knew the whole story—by their smiles! Their smiles were like tracks they left for her to see. Have you left any smile tracks lately?

Once I saw a man I thought had an ugly face. I asked myself if he could even smile, and if he did, would it change his face for the better or would he look worse? As I passed him I gave a hint of a smile in his direction, and he broke out in the most wonderful toothless smile his ugly face could give. It was beautiful.

Try giving someone a smile today and watch them smile back. Leave a smile track—you'll be happier for it, and so will everyone else!

Close with prayer.

DAY 5:

Activity: Kids love a challenge. Use a watch with a second hand and ask the kids to do as many chest pats, knee knocks, and alternate eye blinks as possible in 20 seconds.

Story: Read the story of the Dark Day (p. 93).

Close with prayer.

DAY 6:

Activity: See who can build the tallest tower of mini shredded wheat biscuits in 45 seconds without the tower falling. Winner gets to eat the biscuits!

Story: Read "The First Skyscraper," found in *The Bible Story,* volume 1, page 124.

Close with prayer.

Fascinating Quizzories

Here are quizzes with stories and activities to make the point stick!

2

23. Who Am I?
Three-Second Bible Quiz

Instructions: *Name the first player who will answer. If the player can't answer in three seconds, the question goes to the next player.*

I worshipped frogs. *(Pharaoh)*
I loved to garden. *(Cain)*
I saw a bush on fire. *(Moses)*
I asked my family to help me cut wood. *(Noah)*
I love bad kids. *(Jesus)*
I explained some weird dreams to some prisoners. *(Joseph)*
I carried a sharp knife up a mountain. *(Abraham)*
I had to spend time in jail for something I didn't do. *(Joseph)*
I saw the first rainbow. *(Noah)*
I carried stones down from the top of a mountain. *(Moses)*
I watched animals I'd never seen before. *(Adam)*
I heard an animal speak. *(Balaam)*
I was killed for doing what I was told to do. *(Abel)*
I was told what God was going to do to Pharaoh. *(Moses)*
I picked up a city's security system. *(Samson)*
I had my family move to the nation where I lived. *(Joseph)*
I made lunch for some hungry people. *(Jesus)*
I had dreams of strange, never-before-seen beasts. *(Daniel, John)*
I was the animal that jogged Peter's short memory. *(cock or rooster)*
I used a small stone to make a large man fall down. *(David)*
I asked what they'd give me to betray Jesus. *(Judas)*
I made a door on the side of my boat. *(Noah)*
I chose 12 men to work with Me. *(Jesus)*
I helped my daughter-in-law get a rich husband. *(Naomi)*
I had a valuable slave whom Jesus healed. *(the centurion)*
I badly wanted a son. *(Hannah)*
I was appointed by God to lead Israel after Moses' death. *(Joshua)*
I had brothers who disliked me. *(Joseph and Jesus)*
I survived certain death in a basket. *(Moses)*
I was told to kill my son. *(Abraham)*
I was the animal sent for by Jesus. *(a donkey)*
I talked to Jesus as He hung on the cross. *(thief)*
I saw a bright light that changed my life forever. *(Saul)*
I was shipwrecked hundreds of miles from home. *(Paul)*
I had fresh fruit for breakfast almost every morning. *(Adam, Eve)*
I told some men I would come back to see them. *(Jesus)*

Good Questions!

Instructions: *A fun way to handle these questions is to photocopy them, cut them apart, place them in a cup, let the kids draw them out one at a time, and have them answer them. There are no wrong answers!*

- What if there were no insects? birds? flowers?
- Would you rather wash the dog, pull weeds, or dry dishes? Why?
- What if someone told you that they could see through your head?
- Do you think there will be bees and wasps in heaven? Why?
- My favorite tropical fruit is _____.
- If I accidentally wore my pajamas to school, my friends would _____.
- I'd like to ask Jesus why He _____.
- One thing I think I do well is _____.
- What would you like to ask someone from another planet?
- What I enjoy most about the Sabbath is _____.
- Do you think this world is about to end? Explain why.
- Three things I'd like to do in heaven are: 1. _____ 2. _____ 3. _____
- If you were given $5,000, what would you do with it?
- Two things I would never do are: 1. _____ 2. _____ Because?
- What I like most about my family is _____.
- The one person I trust most is _____ because _____.
- What do you think our world would be like if God didn't exist?
- If I saw my best friend at school take some drugs, I would _____.
- I think I have a talent for _____.
- Do you think people will swim in the river of life?
- Would you rather sing in the choirs or play in the bands of heaven?
- If I saw my two best friends fighting/stealing at school, I would _____.
- Name two things you like about water.
- How would you feel if your sins could never be forgiven?
- Describe an animal you've never seen that could exist in heaven.
- What if Jesus hadn't died on the cross?
- If flowers in heaven never die, what happens to them?
- My second most favorite animal is a _____. Why?

Make up your own questions. Kids never get tired of giving their ideas, and it always provides wonderful interaction with adults.

Fascinating Quizzories

25 What Would You Do?

Instructions: *Kids love situation questions. Try these conversation starters for your next worship.*

1. **You think you see** your best friend cheat on a test at school. WWYD?

   ☐ Ask him/her about it. ☐ Tell the teacher. ☐ Keep quiet. ☐ Tell your friends about it.

2. **Your neighbor asks** you to go to church with him or her next Sunday. WWYD?

   ☐ Go. ☐ Pray about it. ☐ Tell him or her about the Bible Sabbath. ☐ all of these

3. **You find $10** on the floor at school. WWYD?

   ☐ Take it to the principal's office. ☐ Put it in your pocket. ☐ Put it in the offering plate at church.

4. **Your friend tells** a nasty story at school and tells you not to repeat it to anyone else. WWYD?

   ☐ Tell the teacher. ☐ Don't tell anyone. ☐ Tell the story to someone else. ☐ Tell your mom.

5. **The neighbor boy gets** mad and hits you really hard. WWYD?

   ☐ Hit him back. ☐ Say unkind words to him. ☐ Tell your friends about it behind his back. ☐ other

6. **Your good friend invites** you to play ball with him on Sabbath. WWYD?

   ☐ Tell him you'll be in church. ☐ Tell him he's a sinner. ☐ Give him a spiritual magazine.

7. **You find** some dirty pictures on the playground at school. WWYD?

   ☐ Show your mom. ☐ Give them to the teacher. ☐ Throw them in the trash. ☐ Show a friend.

8. **A friend invites** you home for lunch. Her mom serves pork. WWYD?

   ☐ Try it. ☐ Tell her you're a vegetarian. ☐ Go home. ☐ Don't say anything. ☐ Eat only dessert. ☐ other.

9. **A girl tells** you she doesn't like people your color. WWYD?

   ☐ Tell her you don't like her, either. ☐ Pray for her. ☐ Tell the teacher. ☐ Push her down.

10. **You have a friend** who smokes and who invites you to take a puff, just once. WWYD?

    ☐ Take a puff. ☐ Tell them it's not good for them. ☐ Tell your dad. ☐ Don't talk to them.

11. **Two people in** your classroom say they don't like you. WWYD?

    ☐ Try to be friends anyway. ☐ Ask them why. ☐ Never speak to them. ☐ Cry.

12. **You want to go roller skating** with your friends. Your mom says no. WWYD?

    ☐ Just let it go. ☐ Argue with her. ☐ Disappear for a few hours. ☐ Go anyway.

13. **Your dad asks** you to wash the dog. You say OK, but don't. He gets upset. WWYD?

    ☐ Apologize. ☐ Wash the dog. ☐ Tell him you forgot. ☐ Ask your sister to do it.

14. **The score is tied.** You strike out. Angry teammates blame you for losing. WWYD?

    ☐ Tell them it's not important. ☐ Blame the umpire. ☐ Quit the team. ☐ Admit they're right.

15. **Your neighbor asks** you to pick up her dog from the veterinarian next Friday night. WWYD?

    ☐ Ignore her. ☐ Say OK, but don't do it. ☐ Pick up the dog. ☐ Ask a friend to do it.

16. **You have two "friends"** whom a third friend says are saying bad things about you behind your back. WWYD?

    ☐ Talk to each one individually about the rumor. ☐ Report them to the teacher. ☐ Let it go.

17. **A neighbor boy asks to** "borrow" your iPhone, but a whole day later he hasn't returned it. He says he lost it. WWYD?

    ☐ Invite him over for supper to discuss the problem. ☐ Tell your father. ☐ Tell his mother. ☐ Ask him to buy you another one. ☐ Be patient until he finds it.

Big-time Smart and Rich Guy
Open Bible Quiz / 2 Chronicles 9:1-30

Instructions: *An open-Bible look at the world's all-time smartest and richest man*

1. Who came to visit Solomon and why? *(verse 1)*

2. What did she bring as a gift for him? *(verse 9)*

3. What did the servants of Huram bring for Solomon? *(verse 10)*

4. What did Solomon do with the gift of algum wood? *(verse 11)*

5. How much did the gold that came to Solomon each year weigh? *(verse 13)* (About 25 tons, or 56,000 pounds [one ton of gold = 2,240 pounds].)

6. What did he build out of ivory? *(verse 17)*

7. What did Solomon make from the gold? *(verses 15, 16)*

8. Of what did he make his throne? *(verse 17)*

9. What stood beside the arms of Solomon's throne? *(verse 18)*

10. What did Solomon's ships bring him every three years? *(verse 21)*

11. Why did other kings wish to see Solomon? *(verses 23, 24)*

12. How did Solomon get so smart? *(verse 23)*

13. What was as common as stones in Jerusalem? *(verse 27)*

14. How long did Solomon reign in Jerusalem? *(verse 30)*

King David: Good Guy or Bad Guy?

Instructions: *Open your Bibles and decide for yourselves.*

1. Name three instruments used when moving the ark to Jerusalem *(1 Chronicles 15:28)*
2. What was the name of the Levites' musical director? *(verse 22)*
3. What gift did David give to everyone at the time the ark was moved? *(1 Chronicles 16:3)*
4. What did the Lord give David everywhere he went? *(1 Chronicles 18:13)*
5. Who was Hanun? *(1 Chronicles 19:1)*
6. How did David intend to treat Hanun and why? *(verse 2)*
7. How did Hanun treat David's servants? *(verse 4)*
8. What did David do about Hanun's mistreatment? *(verses 6-8)*
9. What did David take from Milcom? *(1 Chronicles 20:2)*
10. What was Goliath's brother's name? *(verse 5)*
11. What was so unusual about one of the giants that warred against David? *(verse 6)*
12. What did David do that displeased God? *(1 Chronicles 21:2, 7)*
13. What was the number of people in Israel? *(verse 5)*
14. What were the three punishments God offered David? *(verses 10-12)*
15. What punishment did David choose, and why? *(verse 13)*
16. What happened to Israel because of David's bad decision? *(verse 14)*
17. Who stopped the killing of the soldiers? *(verse 15)*
18. What did David see hovering in midair, and what did his leaders do? *(verse 16)*
19. What did David do, and what was his suggestion to God? *(verse 17)*
20. What did God tell the prophet Gad to direct David to do? *(verse 18)*
21. What did David ask to buy from Gad and for what purpose? *(verse 22)*
22. What did Gad offer to give David? *(verse 23)*
23. What was David's response to Gad's generous offer? *(verse 24)*
24. How much did David pay Gad? *(verse 25)*
25. How did David know God had heard his prayer? *(verse 26)*
26. What did the angel do at God's command? *(verse 27)*
27. What did David ask the priests to do? *(verse 28)*
28. Was David afraid of anything? If so, of what? *(verse 30)*
29. Would you say that David was a good guy or bad guy? Explain.

28

Plagues and Promises
An Open-Bible Mini Quiz

Earth's Final Days—and Beyond

1. How many groups of people will there be at the end of the world? (Revelation 22:11)
2. What two things did John say God's last-day people would keep? (Revelation 12:17)
3. Name three signs Jesus said we could look for before He returns. (Matthew 24:4-7) Do we see any of these signs today?
4. What did Jesus say the Pharisees could not interpret? (Matthew 16:3)
5. God will send seven plagues upon the wicked. Name two of them. (Revelation 16:2, 3)
6. Where will Jesus appear and how many will see Him? (Revelation 1:7)
7. Name three more plagues mentioned in Revelation 16:4, 8, and 10.
8. What will happen to those who have already died? (1 Thessalonians 4:16)
9. Name the last two of seven plagues mentioned by John. (Revelation 16:12, 17)
10. Where is Satan during all of this? (Revelation 20:1, 2)
11. Where are God's people and what are they doing? (verse 4)
12. What will Satan try to do after 1,000 years of confinement? (verse 7)
13. What did John say would be remade? (Revelation 21:1)
14. What will God's people never experience again? (verse 4)
15. Who says all these things are true? (verses 5, 6)
16. What does Alpha and Omega mean? (verse 6)

Answers: 1. Two. 2. Commandments of God and the faith of Jesus. 3. False messiahs, wars, rumors of wars, famines, earthquakes, etc. 4. Signs of the times. 5. Foul, painful sores; sea turned to blood. 6. In the clouds; every eye shall see Him. 7. Rivers and streams turn to blood; sun scorches the earth; darkness. 8. The dead in Christ will rise from their tombs. 9. River Euphrates dries up; lightning and earthquakes. 10. In a pit. 11. Brought to life and judging. 12. Try to deceive the nations and gather them for battle. 13. The earth. 14. Death, crying, pain. 15. The Alpha and Omega (God). 16. The first and the last.

Purposeful Nature Walks

A walk in nature should be more than just a meaningless stroll.
Put some purpose to it and watch the kids come running.

3

Finding God in Nature

Instructions: *Find God in nature, not just stuff. Fill out this form as you walk. Discover a spiritual lesson from each thing you come across, then show and share for family worship.*

1. What I found _____
2. What it was doing or where it was growing _____
3. My spiritual lesson _____

1. What I found _____
2. What it was doing or where it was growing _____
3. My spiritual lesson _____

1. What I found _____
2. What it was doing or where it was growing _____
3. My spiritual lesson _____

1. What I found _____
2. What it was doing or where it was growing _____
3. My spiritual lesson _____

1. What I found _____
2. What it was doing or where it was growing _____
3. My spiritual lesson _____

1. What I found _____
2. What it was doing or where it was growing _____
3. My spiritual lesson _____

Hands-on Nature Walk

Instructions: *Challenge everyone to notice one thing they've never seen before.*

- **Do** something nice for the squirrels and birds—sprinkle a little dried corn around as you walk.
- **Watch** a bumble bee carefully move among flowers.
- **Collect** a red or red and yellow leaf.
- **Find** a stump and count the rings. Count again and see how big the tree was at your current age.
- **Carve** three "nails" like those used to nail Jesus' feet and hands to the cross.
- **Find** a rock with a line in it.
- **Find** something that has spots on it.
- **Collect** a pinecone or bone.
- **Lie** on your back for one minute and watch the clouds roll by.
- **Find** a tree or stick that has a 90-degree angle ("L").
- **Form** the word "C R E A T O R" with sticks and/or rocks.
- **Make** a unique flower arrangement out of dried weeds, rocks, and wood.
- **Find** a mushroom, cut it in half, and notice the gills under the cap. Use a magnifying glass to see even more.
- **Measure** off with masking tape a 12" x 12" space on the ground and list how many things are living within that space.
- **Discover** how sin has changed God's original creation, and name what evil best describes that activity. Examples: vines taking over a tree: selfishness; aggressiveness. Worms eating a leaf: destruction; wastefulness.
- **Put** water in a transparent glass from a stream or lake and see if there is any living thing visible when you hold it up to the sunlight.
- **Tear** apart a decaying stump and discover what creatures call it home.

Bring home a report of your findings and experiences and share them during your family's sundown worship, then read the first part of The Bible Story, *volume 1, about the creation of the world.*

Sabbath Senses Walk

Instructions: *Carefully scope out where each of these stations will take place. When ready, walk to each site with the family and enjoy doing the things shown below. Each example is intentionally brief, but expand as time allows.*

SOUND

- Sing several songs together—simple instruments optional.
- Whistle a tune together. Listen for the echo.
- Create a whistling noise by blowing a leaf placed between fingers and palm.
- Crush a dried leaf. Bang on a hollow tree. Listen to running water. Shake a dried seed pod.
- Remain silent; listen to nature for one minute. Then, if you can, imitate any of the sounds you heard.

  Before moving on, thank the Lord for the gift of hearing.

SIGHT

- Find brightly colored leaves or other natural things and arrange them in chromatic order.
- Divide into teams of two or three and create a Bible story scene using rocks, sticks, leaves, dirt, etc. Other teams then guess the story depicted.
- Before moving on, thank the Lord for the gift of sight.

TOUCH

- Blindfold the kids, then hand them things to touch. Let them describe what they felt, then guess what it was. Examples: rough, sharp, fuzzy, smooth, wet, hard, soft, slippery, etc.
- Wade barefoot in water.
- Make a thumbprint on a dry rock with a wet thumb.
- Before moving on, thank the Lord for the gift of touch.

SMELL

- Blindfold the kids, then bring things from the woods that have a specific odor and let the kids try to guess the source. Examples: crushed pine needles, rotting wood, mushroom (mold), flowers, mint, etc. (Note: You might wish to bring some things to include here, such as orange peel, soap, bananas, cinnamon, etc.) Be creative.

Before moving on, thank the Lord for the gift of smell.

WORSHIP

- We interrupted our senses walk to have a short spiritual lesson.
- Find three sticks as visual aids: a flat one that can lie on the ground like a worm; a four-pronged one that can stand on all fours like an animal; and a forked stick that stands upright like a person. Place each stick on the ground as you emphasize each point. Explain that Satan has tried to steal God's honor through the theory of evolution, claiming that we evolved from worms to apes, but that God made humans intelligent, upright beings, created in His image.
- Gather in a circle and give thanks for a caring God.

TASTE

- We used our dinner together to enjoy our sense of taste—preceded, of course, by a prayer of gratitude for both gifts of food and taste.
- Dinner table discussion question: Animals have the same senses. What makes humanity different from the other animals?

Purposeful Nature Walks

32 Unzip Heavenly Themes

This nature walk is a bit labor-intensive, but very fun for the kids.

Instructions: *Fill ziplock bags with the letters (on the next page) and one activity (shown below) in each bag. Place the bags along the path in trees, on rocks, beside logs, behind stumps, etc.—partially hidden but still visible. When the family is ready, head out on this Sabbath discovery walk. Your kids will love hunting for the bags and doing the various activities at each site.*

Bag 1. In each ziplock bag you will find a big letter. The first bag has two letters. Collect all 10 letters. They will form a puzzle. At the end of the walk we will put them in order. *Find the next clue.*

Bag 2. Read Revelation 21:10-13, 16, 21. Here is a description of the Holy City. Draw in the sand, or form with sticks, an outline of this city; create its temple, use stones as gates and small leaves as angel guards. *Next clue.*

Bag 3. Collect water from a stream or lake in this plastic bag. Is it perfectly clear, or did it have something alive? Hold it up to the sun and look again. What do you see? Do you think heaven's rivers will have unseen life? *Next clue.*

Bag 4. Collect six to eight sticks. Break them into any size you need to form them into an object or thing you will use or see in heaven. Example: house, shelf, crown, pet, etc.

Bag 5. Using your name as an acrostic, name things from each letter that you look forward to seeing in the new earth. *Next clue.*

Bag 6. Have everyone sit down; then have someone read a short story about heaven. (We used *My Bible Friends*.) *Next clue.*

Bag 7. The Bible says there was silence in heaven for about a half hour (Revelation 8:1). Why? Remain silent for one minute. *Next clue.*

Bag 8. Find in this bag two cutout pictures made of multiple-angled cuts. This is a puzzle. Make them into two separate pictures again. You'll discover that one picture is of things we will find in heaven, and the other of things we won't see there. Explain your pictures and answers. *Next clue.*

Bag 9. Collect the green letters and place them in order to find the name of something we'll find in heaven. The first letter is T. The final clue is found in Revelation 22:2. *Next clue.*

Bag 10. Find a large tree for all to gather under and imagine that it is the tree of life. End with prayer that you and your family will gather together under this tree and eat of its delicious fruit.

Clue: The boldface letter is the first letter for something we'll find in heaven. What do the letters spell?

Interactive Family Worship Ideas for Kids

TIFR
EOE
FLE

33 Walkin' With the Word

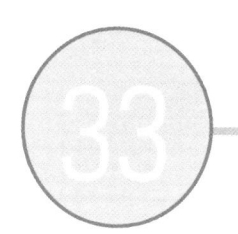

Instructions: *This worship walk is in two parts. First, have the kids look up the key words from the texts supplied (first letter given). The answers become the list of things to look for on your walk. Give five points for every item found, and five points if shown for the evening worship. Use* The Clear Word *paraphrase.*

SCRIPTURE CLUE	FIND AND SHOW
Matthew 13:32	☐ s _ _ _
Jonah 2:10	☐ f _ _ _
Proverbs 6:6	☐ a _ _
Psalm 50:11	☐ b _ _ _
Jeremiah 2:13	☐ w _ _ _ _
Ezekiel 37:7	☐ b _ _ _
Matthew 6:19	☐ r _ _ _
John 15:2	☐ b _ _ _ _ _
Jonah 4:6	☐ v _ _ _
Jeremiah 18:6	☐ c _ _ _
Psalm 91:1	☐ s _ _ _ _ _
Acts 1:9	☐ c _ _ _ _
Genesis 2:19	☐ a _ _ _ _ _
Genesis 1:11	☐ g _ _ _ _
Exodus 10:4	☐ l _ _ _ _ _
Psalm 119:105	☐ p _ _ _
Matthew 27:33	☐ s _ _ _ _
Mark 15:17	☐ t _ _ _ _
1 Samuel 2:2	☐ r _ _ _
Genesis 8:8	☐ d _ _ _
Isaiah 66:20	☐ h _ _ _ _ _
Luke 6:44	☐ f _ _ _ _
Luke 19:40	☐ s _ _ _ _ _
Psalm 18:11	☐ c _ _ _ _
Matthew 12:33	☐ t _ _ _

Matthew 13:32, seed; Jonah 2:10, fish; Proverbs 6:6, ant; Psalm 50:11, bird; Jeremiah 2:13, water; Ezekiel 37:7, bone; Matthew 6:19, rust; John 15:2, branch; Jonah 4:6, vine; Jeremiah 18:6, clay; Psalm 91:1, shadow; Acts 1:9, cloud; Genesis 2:19, animal; Genesis 1:11, grass; Exodus 10:4, locust (grasshopper); Psalm 119:105, path; Matthew 27:33, skull; Mark 15:17, thorn; 1 Samuel 2:2, rock; Genesis 8:8, dove; Isaiah 66:20, horses; Luke 6:44, fruit; Luke 19:40, stones; Psalm 18:11, cloud; Matthew 12:33, tree

Spoken Like a Tree

34

Instructions: *As you walk, find trees that could be described by the words in the right column, then find the text that uses the same word. Draw a line between the two. (Use* The Clear Word *paraphrase.)*

Ecclesiastes 3:11	☐	☐	beginning
Luke 3:5	☐	☐	bent down
Luke 24:23	☐	☐	tree of life
Ezekiel 31:3	☐	☐	two
Deuteronomy 4:31	☐	☐	wrapped
Proverbs 4:5	☐	☐	death
Daniel 6:26	☐	☐	smooth
1 Corinthians 15:26	☐	☐	beautiful
Zechariah 3:8	☐	☐	reach out
Proverbs 3:18	☐	☐	awesome
Hosea 11:4	☐	☐	cut off
Psalm 47:2	☐	☐	branch
Romans 11:21	☐	☐	rough
Luke 3:5	☐	☐	abandon
Luke 2:7	☐	☐	alive
Exodus 31:18	☐	☐	living

Purposeful Nature Walks

35 Secret Word Walk

WORD LIST:

rest	music	holy
gift	walk	nature
enjoy	Creation	servant

1. Before the walk, an adult will select a secret word and have the kids draw or cut out large letters from magazines to form that word. However, only the adult will know what the word is. Choose such words as the ones in the word list. (I suggest you avoid words that use the same letter more than once, such as sabbath.) Keep the letters in an easy-to-carry container and take them on your walk.

2. As you walk, let the kids draw out one letter and find things that begin with that letter. After a few minutes, pull out another letter, etc. Save all the objects and the letters.

3. At the end of the walk, spread out what you have found, including the letters, and briefly discuss each item. Are there any object lessons that you can draw from anything you've seen or found?

4. Ask if anyone can guess the surprise word before you ceremoniously arrange the letters on the table into the secret word you've chosen. Discuss the word.

5. Close with a song and a prayer.

Send Them Out!
Take the Challenge!

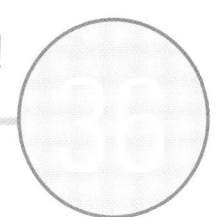

See how many missionaries you can send out!

Secure a world map. Find Switzerland and briefly review other countries around the world. Let the kids find three other countries or islands where they would like to send a missionary. Tag their selection on the map with a sticky, then write the countries on a card and place them upside down in a stack. Shuffle the cards. Players will draw a card from the stack to determine where their "missionary" will go.

Place a basket about five feet away (distance varies with skill level) and let the players try to toss a balloon into the basket. If they succeed, they will have "sent" their missionary to that country. If they miss the basket, continue to the next player.

Object: See how many missionaries you can send out.

Close by reading the story of John Nevins Andrews (p. 88), then discuss what it must be like to be a missionary in a foreign land. Have a special prayer for the many missionaries serving Jesus all around the world.

God's Amazing Laws

Instructions: *This is a very challenging walk that calls for close observation, but you'll discover nature's laws are everywhere—we just don't often take note of them. Write these laws down as you go.*

Such laws as:
    Trees grow up, roots grown down.
    Water runs downhill.
    Vapor rises (becoming clouds).
    Sunlight dries things.
    Seeds sprout.
    Wind blows everywhere, but can never be seen.
    The cycle of life: seed, sprout, grow, bloom, death, seed, etc.

You and your child will enjoy finding many more. At the end of your discovery walk, review your list and discuss the importance of these laws. Then explain that God's moral laws for His people are also important. Next read His moral laws from Exodus 20:3-17. Review your findings with the whole family.

This will definitely be time well spent, and your kids will love the challenge.

Follow the Marshmallow Trail

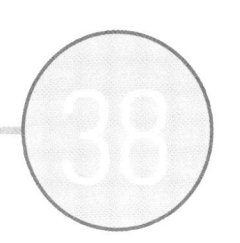

Here's a sweet way to get your family from sleepy time to worship time and enjoy the journey. Scope out a trail to a nice location for worship. Then go back and mark the trail by randomly dropping small marshmallows along the path to the worship site. (Spacing should be age-appropriate.) Tell the kids to follow the "marshmallow trail" until they find the designated site. Be sure to include some "Y"s and some "T"s in the trail that lead to dead ends, as well as some wide circles that ultimately lead back to the main trail. Kids will love the hunt. Close with a story from *My Bible Friends* and a short prayer, and enjoy a few marshmallows!

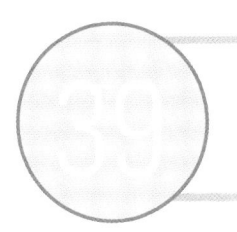

The Imperfect Example
How Did Perfect Become Imperfect?

Instructions: *Mark two paper bags: one with the word* Perfect, *the other* Imperfect. *During the walk everybody will be looking for both perfect and imperfect leaves. The perfect leaves are flawless while the imperfect ones have damage from insects, brown spots, age, or whatever. Have the kids crush the imperfect bag into a ball, then open it back up and smooth it out. (It will never be perfect again.)*

As you walk along, have the kids find leaves in each category and place them in the appropriate bag. At the end of the walk, select an example from each of the two bags that best fits the description (perfect or imperfect), then ask these thought questions:

Thought Questions:
Which bag was it easier to find leaves for? Why?
Why have some things been damaged?
Who destroyed them?
Do you think the cause of such imperfection should be destroyed?
Is that fair?
Who made things perfect?
The leaves in the "perfect" bag are no longer perfect because they have now been picked and will die. Can you think of anything in the Bible that was perfect but had to die? (*sacrificial lamb*) Was that fair?

Can you think of anyone in the Bible who was perfect but had to die? Was that fair? How does that make you feel?

Purposeful Nature Walks

Simon Sharp-eye
Nature Observer

40

Instructions: *Before you start on a nature walk, go over this list of nature items that you might find in your area, and assign a numerical value to each one based on how likely it is to be seen. That number becomes the number of points your kids earn when they spot the item (sample points appear after each item suggested). Total them at the end of the walk.*

TO COLLECT:	POINTS
☐ pinecone, *1 point*	_____
☐ feather, *2 points*	_____
☐ snakeskin, *10 points*	_____
☐ mushroom, *2 points*	_____
☐ caterpillar, *3 points*	_____
☐ blue flower, *3 points*	_____
☐ woodpecker nest, *4 points*	_____
☐ red leaf, *2 points*	_____
☐ sweet gum ball, *2 points*	_____
☐ woven bird nest, *7 points*	_____
☐ dragonfly, *5 points*	_____
☐ moss, *4 points*	_____
☐ shell, *3 points*	_____
☐ snail, *5 points*	_____
☐ cocoon, *8 points*	_____
☐ moth, *3 points*	_____
☐ paper hornet's nest, *8 points*	_____
☐ cattail, *3 points*	_____
☐ four-leaf clover, *20 points*	_____
☐ butterfly, *3 points*	_____
☐ acorn with cap, *4 points*	_____
☐ _____	_____
☐ _____	_____
☐ _____	_____
☐ _____	_____
☐ _____	_____
☐ _____	_____
	TOTAL _____

Note: The first to reach 50 points gets to wear the Simon Sharp-eye Badge of Honor and will show and tell something about their discoveries for the evening worship.

SIMON SHARP-EYE BADGE OF HONOR

SPYING

AWARDED TO

_____

for being a careful observer of some of God's most amazing things.

"Their voice goes out through all the earth" (Psalm 19:4, NRSV).

Five Stations Walk

With Rhyming Clues to Keep Us Guessing

This was an enjoyable vacation Sabbath in place of a formal church service. Part of the fun was watching the kids figure out where the next clue was taking them. You will need to scope out your own area and create your own clues and rhymes, but it's a fun approach to Sabbath worship in the woods.

Items to purchase in advance:
Clay for everyone *(station 1)*
Balloons prestuffed with texts *(station 2)*
Plastic bags *(station 3)*
Gum *(prize for station 4)*

Station 1:

Clue: It's round and tall and loaded with power; it's east of here, less than an hour. *(telephone pole)*

Activity: Mold a piece of clay so that it looks like a person or animal. Name it and pretend that it's good for something *(brings rain, cures headache, etc.)*

Read: Exodus 20:4-6

Ask: Does my "creature" really have any such ability? Can it do anything at all? Could you worship something you've made? (Some people have!) Why did God tell us not to worship idols? Do we have idols today? What might they be?

Station 2:

Clue: It's long and soft and anchored in a tree; a great place to be when you're lazy. *(hammock)*

Activity: Pass out balloons to everyone, blow them up, then pop them. Read the surprise text hiding inside each balloon. (Note: Before the game started, I placed a text with a promise inside each balloon.)

Read: the text in each balloon

Discuss: the meaning of each text.

Station 3:

Clue: It's quiet when alone but squeaks when it's moved; no trespasser is ever confused. *(iron gate)*

Read: Genesis 1

Activity: Creation scavenger hunt. Break into teams of two or more and scatter to find objects connected with each day of creation. Return and show the group what you have found and explain the reasoning behind each selection. (Note: Day 1: light. Day 2: atmosphere. Day 3: dry land from water. Day 4: sun, moon, stars. Day 5: fish, birds. Day 6: animals, man. Day 7: Sabbath.)

Station 4:

Clue: It once was man's shiny slave, but today rust is taking it to its grave. *(old truck)*

Activity: Bible charades with a twist. Four teams will spread out and create mini scenes of the story of David and Goliath. Use only sticks, stones, and sounds—*not words!* Vote on the best, and the winning team gets a prize!

Station 5:

Clue: There are no coins in its banks, but there are rocks in its bed! *(down by the stream)*

Read: Joshua 4:1-7

Activity: Build a monument to the Sabbath. Find 12 large stones from the streambed and bring them to the site selected. Stack them into a monument, creating a memorial to God's holy day. Briefly discuss its significance. End with a prayer of thanks for the Sabbath.

Purposeful Nature Walks

Quiet Worship Ideas

Here is a collection of short worship ideas that you can enjoy in the quiet of your living room.

4

Charations
Variations on Family Charades

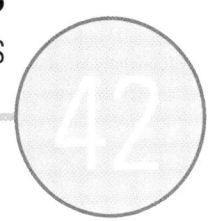

42

Instructions: *Kids love Bible charades—try these variations:*
1. Set up a sheet in front of a light and let the actor create the story from the shadow between the light and the screen.
2. Use sock or real puppets to act out your Bible story for the family.
3. Read the text first, then let the kids act out the story.
4. Let the kids act out the story as you slowly read it line for line.
5. Let the kids find and read a story for someone else to act out.

A few texts to get you started:
Acts 16:25-34	Acts 12:5-18
Joshua 6:1-27	1 Kings 13
1 Kings 17 and 18	Luke 15:22-24

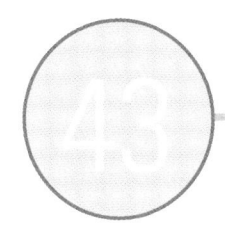

43

Define the Line

You might be surprised at how much your kids know—or don't know—about their church. Take this challenge in your next worship.

Instructions: *Rewrite or enlarge each of the following words and place them faceup on the floor or table. Let each player select a word, then in turn explain its meaning to the family. This will generate some interesting worship discussion and educate everyone. Make up other church or Bible words as you play.*

Old Testament
Holy Spirit
Second Coming
Godhead
hallowed
New Testament
temperance

Advent
holy
Seventh-day Adventist
conference
union, division
General Conference

44 Spiritual or Physical Light

The word "light" appears throughout Scripture. In some settings it means physical light, while other times it refers to spiritual knowledge or understanding. This can be confusing. Let's let the kids look up those texts and figure out which is which.

Genesis 1:16	☐ spiritual	☐ physical
Genesis 1:3-5	☐ spiritual	☐ physical
Exodus 13:21	☐ spiritual	☐ physical
2 Corinthians 11:14	☐ spiritual	☐ physical
Romans 13:12	☐ spiritual	☐ physical
Matthew 2:9, 10	☐ spiritual	☐ physical
John 1:9	☐ spiritual	☐ physical
John 8:12	☐ spiritual	☐ physical
James 1:17	☐ spiritual	☐ physical
Isaiah 9:2	☐ spiritual	☐ physical
Matthew 4:16	☐ spiritual	☐ physical
Isaiah 60:1	☐ spiritual	☐ physical
Revelation 22:5	☐ spiritual	☐ physical

"Then God said, 'Let there be light.'"

"I am the light of the world."

Sunlight or Artificial Light?

Just as there is a difference between spiritual and physical light, so there are differences between sunlight and artificial light. God made them both, of course, but here are some interesting facts about both that you might not have known.

The ***sunlight*** that we see every day travels at the incredible rate of 186,282 miles per second. At that speed we could circle the earth more than seven times in a single second! Light takes just a little more than eight minutes to travel from the sun to the tip of your nose.

While sunlight seems to be clear, it is actually very colorful. Humans can see red, orange, yellow, green, blue indigo, and violet in a rainbow. Each color vibrates at its own wavelength. Cool colors like blue and green have short wavelengths, while warm colors like yellow and red have longer wavelengths.

Sunlight is better for us than artificial light. Neither humans nor animals nor plants could exist without sunlight. Sunlight aids in the migration of birds. It causes leaves to turn green, and even produces vitamin D in our bodies. The sun is an awesome gift of light and energy that God personally created for our world, and it's still burning bright!

Artificial light is human-made light. It does not radiate a complete spectrum of colors. Instead it produces an excess of one or more of the color rays. Scientists have found that both natural and artificial light affect animals and plants, but in very different ways. Here are some examples:

An experiment on mice discovered that they produced the same number of male as female babies when exposed to sunlight, but under artificial light more female babies than males were born. It was also found that their babies did not do as well under artificial light, and that the adults died earlier than those exposed to sunlight. (*Wikipedia*)

Plants don't live very well under artificial light either. They are not as sturdy as those grown in God's natural sunlight. Apples grew larger but did not ripen, and the fruit never acquired full color until exposed to the rays of the sun. (*Wikipedia*)

Light brings happiness and peace to everyone. It is just another free gift that God gives us. Let's remember to thank Him every day. God's gifts are the best.

Heavenly Senses

46

Instructions: *Photocopy these cards and place them upside down on the table. Each player will draw a card and tell what he or she would like to (1) (for example, "see") in heaven for the first time, and (2) what they will be glad to never have to (for example, "see") again from this world. Mix the cards up and go around several times. Redraw if you get the same thing twice. It should become creative. The five senses:* **see, feel, hear, taste, smell.**

68   Interactive Family Worship Ideas for Kids

Creating My Very Own . . .

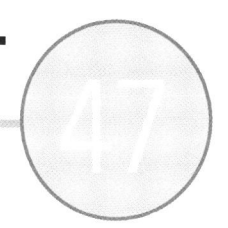

Instructions: *Wouldn't it be fun to create a new, never-before-seen animal? Will it be a bird, an insect, or a mammal? You decide—but not until you create it. Here's how:*

Take an oval leaf, a rock, or even some moss and smear it across an ink pad, then carefully stamp it on a plain piece of paper. Now add some whiskers or legs or ears if you like and kazaam! you are the first to ever see a _____ (name it). Now tell me more:

My _____ is a _____ and lives in a _____. It likes to eat _____, which is why it has _____. It doesn't like to be _____, but it loves for me to _____.

This one is about as big as a _____ and its color is _____. Sometimes they like to _____, but only if there is enough _____ around, or if they can find other _____. Notice the _____ on their back and legs, which helps them _____. I would like to see one of these in heaven, where my _____ and I could _____ with them every day. I would love to show it to Jesus and have Him tell me about its _____ and how He created everything.

Quiet Worship Ideas

Want to Be a Missionary?

48

Instructions: *You want to be a missionary, but you're not sure what you could do? Here are some ideas and conversation starters.* **Put a star beside your top five ideas from the left column,** *then draw a line to the "jobs I would consider" as appropriate. Use colored pencils so that you can easily see the lines when you review them in family worship.*

Things I Like to Do	Jobs I Would Consider
I like to teach	Grow food
I like to build things	Heal diseases
I like to fly airplanes	Preach
I love music	Be a doctor or nurse
I like to watch things grow	Build greenhouses
I like to draw	Help at summer camp or VBS
I love math	Be a plumber, carpenter, or welder
I like to care for people	Draw/design for magazines/books
I like to be in charge	Operate a hospital
I like athletic things	Be a principal
I like to make things	Be an archaeologist
I like to explore	Be a well driller
I like people	Be a librarian
I like computer stuff	Fly an airplane for missionaries
I like to read my Bible	Build churches, schools, clinics
I love kids	Sell Christian books and magazines
I like animals	Be a veterinarian
I love to give advice	Help cure drug addictions
I like to dig in the ground	Run a printing press
I like photography	Be an accountant or banker
I like to read	Be a teacher
I like medical stuff	Be a computer technician
I like to work with my hands	Be a choir and/or band director
I like to be outdoors	Be a gym teacher

Every Person a Worker

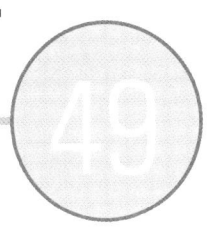

Instructions: *Ancient Hebrew tradition decreed that every boy learn a trade. Here are some Bible trades. See if you can put names or texts with them:*

gardener_____	miners_____
carpenter_____	potter_____
tentmaker_____	tanner_____
boatbuilder_____	timber cutters_____
brickmakers_____	weavers_____
masons_____	gold artisan_____
metalworker_____	shepherd_____

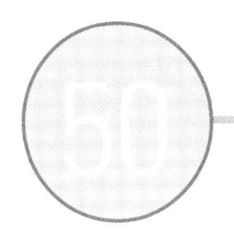

Parable of the Sower
Show and Tell—Sandbox Version

Directions: *Establish a weed-free, sandy area, and let the kids smooth out the sand and help you find and pick a handful of **seeds**,* some small **rocks**, and some very small **leaves** (to suggest birds). Adults cut off a short section of thorns from a nearby bush and place them in the sand.*

Now have the kids arrange the items in the space, sprinkle the tiny seeds randomly throughout the sandbox collage, and add the "birds." Read or tell the story of the parable from Matthew 13:1-9 and explain the parable from verses 18-23.

Hidden Treasure: You might also hide a marble or brightly colored object in the sand and have the kids dig to find it, then tell or read the parable of the hidden treasure in Matthew 13:44.

---

*The best time to find seeds in the wild is late summer. You might also use tiny pebbles to suggest seeds.

Quiet Worship Ideas

51. Making a Blessings Chain

Instructions: Let the kids make a list of things they are thankful for. Have them write them down on small pieces of colored paper. Next let them tape the pieces of paper into a chain that they can read for worship and afterward hang on their bedroom door.

52. Show Me the Fruit

Instructions: Find pictures in old magazines that could represent a fruit of the spirit in action: **love, joy, peace, patience, kindness, goodness, faithfulness.** Glue them on 8½" x 11" sheets of paper and share them with the family at worship time.

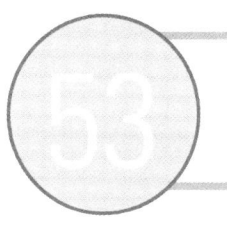

53. Lessons From Inanimate Objects

Instructions: Place an object such as a blackboard eraser, a wrench, a stethoscope, or almost anything that is work-related, in a basket or jar, pass it around for all to see, then ask the following questions one at a time:
1. What makes this tool unique?
2. How could it bring praise to God in my hands?
3. How could I use it to spread the gospel?
4. What spiritual lesson can I draw from it?
5. What uniquely qualifies me for God's service?

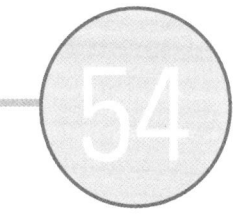

54. Six-Word Story

Instructions: See if you can tell the gist of a Bible story in six words. Example: Eve tempted. Eve ate. Eve died. / Noah built a boat. Family saved.

Build a Story on a Paper Plate

Instructions: *Gather a little sand, some sticks (or toothpicks), small leaves, a few rocks, marbles, a strip of cloth, or whatever, and tell the kids to build a Bible story scene on a plate. (Example: David and Goliath, Israelites marching around Jericho, disciples pulling fish into a boat, etc.) They're creative and imaginative enough to dive in and amaze you and themselves, too. When they've finished, everyone tries to guess the story they've depicted. The kids will squeal with delight to hear your guesses, and rush to tell you the right answer! Then let them tell you the whole story.*

Affirmation Confirmation

Instructions: *Let the family take a few minutes during worship to write a note of thanks and/or appreciation to the pastor, a leader, a senior, or a child in your church and give it to them Sabbath morning. The recipients will never forget your kindness, and you will never forget their smiles.*

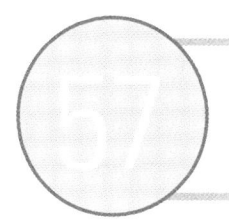

New and Improved

Instructions: *For this worship, have your kids list some physical characteristics generally seen in your family (hair/skin color, big ears, long toes, shape and color of eyes, etc.). Remind the family that someday we are all going to be changed "in a moment, in the twinkling of an eye" (1 Corinthians 15:51).*
    Now ask these thought questions:
- What changes would you like God to make in your body at that time?
- What talent(s) would you like to receive, and why?
- How might you use the new talents to praise Jesus more?
- What deceased family member would you like to meet again, and what family characteristic do you think he or she might still have in heaven?
- What characteristic(s) do you hope God preserves to keep your family line unique?

    Close by reading Revelation 21:24-27; 22:1-5, 20.

Quiet Worship Ideas

58. The Tithe Envelope Worship

Instructions: *Bring home a tithe envelope from church and use the evening's worship to explain the various offerings shown on its cover.*

Explain the concept of tithing.

Explain the other offerings and how the local church, the conference, the union, and the world divisions use them.

Let the kids have the envelope(s) for an offering they might wish to give.

Each one read a portion of Malachi 3:8-12, and close with prayer.

59. Bible Story Goofups!

Instructions: *Explain to the kids that you are going to read (or tell) a common Bible story but intentionally fill it with big mistakes and/or exaggerations. Don't change facial or voice expressions as you read (or tell) but watch the kids jump at every detail and correct your every mistake! See if you can sneak some by them that you can later point out, but confirm with a nod each time they catch one of your changes. They will love this and will listen very carefully!*

60. Envelope Surprise Worship

Instructions: *Write down various worship assignments and place them in envelopes. Without peeking, each member will draw one envelope and take that part of the worship.*

Here are some idea starters:

1. Have opening prayer. 2. Review the family's week. 3. Provide music. 4. Share an object lesson. 5. Give a nature nugget. 6. Have closing prayer. 7. Read or tell a story. 8. Share a blessing. 9. Name something you're thankful for, etc.

Be creative. Give everyone an assignment and a minute to gather their thoughts, then proceed.

Highlights of the Week

Instructions: *Take time during worship to let each person tell*
(1) what highlight they had with someone during the week.
(2) what they learned during the week.
(3) in what way they grew closer to Jesus.
(4) why they are glad it's Sabbath.

Answers could fill an entire family worship. Record this worship, and it will bring volumes of memories in times to come.

Takin' My Family to Heaven

Instructions: *Start by letting the kids name a Bible person beginning with "A," and say "I'm taking my family to heaven and A, too." The next player repeats the phrase and adds another name using the next letter of the alphabet ("B") as the first letter of the next Bible character.*

Example: "I'm taking my family to heaven and **A**dam, too." The next player continues with "I'm taking my family to heaven and **B**oaz, too," etc.

See how many Bible characters you can take to heaven!

Homespun Cinema Fun

This worship has two parts:
1. During the week, let kids draw and color imaginative scenes that show the seven days of creation (or any other Bible story) on 3" x 5" cards. Place the drawings in chronological order and tape them together in one long line.

2. Cut slots on each side of a cardboard box and cut a TV-like screen on the bottom of the box. Let someone thread the taped drawings through the sides of the box one frame at a time, (like a movie) and *voilà!* the whole family can watch and hear the creation story unfold before your eyes while you read it!

Bread of Life

Hands-on Object Lesson Worship

64

Instructions: *Let the kids help make this bread (crackers) recipe before worship. Enjoy the crackers as a part of your evening worship, but use the following as a worship guide. Explain the meanings and bring to mind fresh lessons from this exercise.*

*BREAD OF LIFE CRACKER RECIPE

3 cups old-fashioned oats
3 cups white flour
¾ cup olive oil
1¼ cup water
3 teaspoons salt
3 tablespoons sugar

Combine, roll thin on cookie sheet, score into squares, and bake at 300° F for 30 minutes. (Turn cookie sheet frequently so sides brown evenly.)
Jesus said: "I am the bread of life" (John 6:35).

Activity:

JESUS: WAS BROKEN, beaten, and sifted by Satan.
Kids: *Crush and sift wheat berries into flour (small quantity for effect).*

JESUS: MIXED with the common people to make them better.
Kids: *Mix grains with other ingredients.**

JESUS: WAS TEMPTED and "baked" in the wilderness by Satan.
Kids: *Can feel Satan's heat and remember they are also tempted by him.*

JESUS: CAME FORTH from the dark tomb.
Kids: *Can also be taken from Satan's "hot oven" of temptation.*

JESUS: WENT FORTH to serve humanity.
Kids: *Can serve their friends, too. Name some ways to do this.*

More Than Meets the Ear

This is a *Seventh-day Adventist Hymnal* discovery worship.

From the **Topical Index** (p. 776), select three songs for the family to sing from the Adoration and Praise section.

Using the **Alphabetical Index of Tunes** (p. 816), write in the names of these well-known hymns from these original tune names:

Antioch _____Example: Joy to the World_____ (125)

Bradbury _____ (190)

Coronation _____ (229)

Dennis _____ (350)

Ein' Feste Burg _____ (506)

Finlandia _____ (461)

From the **Composers, Arrangers, and Sources** (p. 813), find these composers and write in the title of the song they wrote.

Ackley, B. D. _____ (311)

Barnes, Edward S. _____ (142)

Luther, Martin _____ (506)

Malan, H.A.C. _____ (330)

Showalter, A. J. _____ (469)

Runyan, William M. _____ (100)

From the **Scriptural Readings** section, read together no. 706, "Let Heaven Praise the Lord." Father and sons will read the light print, while mother and daughters will read the bold print.

66

End-time Museum

This could be an ongoing worship activity with weekly updates added to the "museum" and reported weekly at Friday night worships. Try it for a few weeks or more—you'll be amazed at what you can find.

Instructions: *Gather information from magazines, newspapers, Internet—any source that will confirm that the Bible predictions for the end of the world are coming to pass today. The more information you gather, the more amazing the Bible's accuracy becomes. See how many of the following categories you can find and put on display in your own in-house museum.*

Here are some categories to get you started. Use them as headlines to start each section.

EARTH WEARING OUT
(Isaiah 51:6) _____

EARTHQUAKES, FAMINES, FEAR, PESTILENCE
(Luke 21:11) _____

WARS AND RUMORS OF WARS
(Luke 21:9, 10) _____

KNOWLEDGE INCREASES
(Daniel 12:4) _____

GOSPEL TO ALL THE WORLD
(Matthew 24:14) _____

PEOPLE LOVERS OF SELVES AND MONEY
(2 Timothy 3:1-5) _____

EVOLUTION CONFUSION
(2 Peter 3:3-5; Revelation 14:6, 7) _____

COUNTERFEIT SIGNS AND WONDERS
(Revelation 14:9-12) _____

COMING IN JESUS' NAME
(Luke 21:8) _____

Meaningful Stories

Here are some character-building stories filled with truth and significance that you can use for family worships.

5

67

I Am Me—Who Are You?

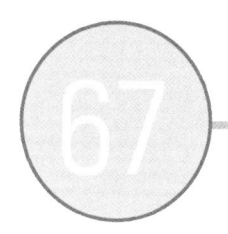

It was Halloween. Johnny was 4. His parents had dressed him in the scariest outfit they could find around the house—Mom's silly-looking church hat, Dad's oversize pants and shoes, and a goofy mask from the drugstore that was twice the size of his face. Nothing was too good for their big boy! They overlooked no detail for his first big "night mission," the object of which was to scare his two young cousins Bob and Bill to within an inch of their lives!

Johnny's cousins lived just down the street at their grandparents' house. So the plan was to drive down to Gram's house after dark, exit the car, and sneak up to the front door. Johnny was to ring the doorbell, and when the cousins opened the door, he was to yell "Boo!" in the scariest voice a 4-year-old could muster. Then everyone would laugh and watch as the two cousins would scream in terror upon seeing this "thing" at their front door. As I said, that was the plan, and it was on!

Johnny was all systems go. As planned, he ran across Gram's big front yard in pants and shoes that were much too big, tripping at every step. And that silly, oversize mask kept sliding down his face and around to the back of his head. But those were minor details, and Johnny and his parents pressed forward through the darkness on their scary mission.

Upon reaching the front door, Johnny waited impatiently until his security units (Mom and Dad) caught up. Then he met a small detail that hadn't been discussed. Quietly peering from the darkness behind the screen door, Johnny saw two of the scariest masked faces he'd ever seen staring back at him! He froze, belted out in terror, then grabbed Dad's big leg and held on tightly, terrified at what might happen next. No one had mentioned that his two cousins might dress up to scare him too! The only plan he knew was to scare them—and it had backfired. The tears flowed, but when they dried and everyone took their masks off, the boys became just cousins once again.

One day Jesus came upon a scary man. He was filthy, naked, and bloody. Broken chains dangled from his wrists, and he came running out from a smelly graveyard right toward Jesus. He fell down and screamed. Any ordinary person would have fled in terror, but Jesus wasn't ordinary. He, like Johnny, held tight to His Father. Then Jesus healed the scary wild man and sent him back to his home to tell his family and friends what Jesus had done for him. Jesus cares for us, too—even when things seem real scary.

Read the story for yourself in Luke 8:26-39.

Why? Is a *Good* Question

"I have a question," Samantha interrupted as the teacher was giving pointers on safety.

"Yes, Samantha?"

"Teacher, you said that we must always walk on the left side of the road? Why?"

"That's correct," Ms. Jones replied. "So you don't have to turn around to see the cars coming."

"Ms. Jones, I'm confused. No matter which side of the road I walk on, I will always have to turn around to see cars coming. So what difference does it make?"

Her teacher smiled and said, "That's a good question, Samantha. I see why you're confused. Let me explain it more clearly. You must walk on the left side of the road so you can more easily see the cars coming *toward* you in *your* lane. It's true that you would have to turn around to see cars coming from behind, but they are not as likely to run into you as those coming toward you in your same lane. Does that help?"

"Yes. Thank you! That makes much more sense," the girl replied.

We are daily bombarded with questions of all kinds. *Why* must I obey everything Mom or Dad says? *Why* must I go to church every week? *Why* can't I have more cookies? It's never wrong to ask *why*. There are almost as many *good* answers as there are *why* questions. But when it comes to questions about rules, we must always obey the rules—even if they don't make sense at the moment.

Eve asked, "Why can't I eat that gorgeous fruit being offered to me? Obviously it hasn't hurt the serpent eating it? Why can't I take just a little bite?" She disobeyed God's rule—*Stay away from the tree*—and we've been living in a world of sin ever since. She didn't understand why, but I'm sure if she could see the misery and destruction that resulted from not obeying God's rule, and if she had a second chance to make the decision again, she would have decided very differently.

It's never wrong to ask *why*, even when God makes rules. But then we must obey His rule, even though we may not fully understand the answer. *Why?* is a good question, and God has the best answers—because no one knows more about us or loves us more than our Creator Himself. What question would you like to ask Him, and why?

In the Palace of a King

Instructions: *What would you do if you found out the king of your country didn't like you and began trying every way possible to kill you, but ended up killing himself instead? Would you want to be king in his place? This actually happened. Here's the story:*

After days and months of fleeing from Saul, David got the news that King Saul had committed suicide while engaged in a violent battle. He had become surrounded by enemy troops, so he chose to kill himself by falling on his own sword rather than be taken captive by his enemies. And not only did Saul die that day, but his three sons perished as well.

So if you had been David, what would you have done? Would you have celebrated Saul's death or mourned his loss?

Then someone remembered what an outstanding soldier David had been, and suggested that he might be the perfect next king. Yes! the crowd roared with approval, and quickly David was elected the new king of the nation.

David and his staff now made all the decisions. And one of them was how to deal with Saul's family, who, just a short time before had wished to kill him. Should he, in order to make his kingdom safe, now kill those who remained, or should he be kind and show himself to be a godly king? WWYD?

Quickly King David sent his staff out to find anyone from Saul's family that he could invite to the palace. Enter Ziba, Saul's former servant. He said that Saul's grandson Mephibosheth still remained alive, but was crippled from a bad fall he'd taken while still a baby. Immediately David sent men to bring Mephibosheth to the palace.

Terrified, Mephibosheth fell on his face before the king, believing that he faced certain death. He a member of Saul's family; he could be seen as someone from the old regime who should be killed. But David kindly assured Mephibosheth that all was well and that he need not be afraid. He said, "I will show you kindness for the sake of your father, Jonathan; I will restore to you all the land of your grandfather Saul, and you shall always eat at my table." Wow! What a kind king.

Then David turned to Saul's servant, Ziba, whom the king could also have killed, and said, "You and your sons shall till the land for Mephibosheth, and shall bring in the produce, so that your master's grandson may have food to eat." Another act of kindness.

So this unusual story has a happy ending, because David was a man of God. And when King David had questions about the right thing to do, he went to God for advice—and *that's what we must always do as well.*

(See 2 Samuel 9:1-11, NRSV.)

An Old Man, a Little Dog, and a Helpful Boy

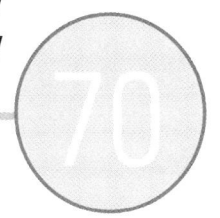

Instructions: *Draw smiley, sad, and angry faces (☺ ☹ 😠) on a Post-it note. Attach each to a Popsicle stick and give both to each kid. As you read the following story, have each child hold up the face they feel best answers the questions you ask. They can use the sad face for anger or fear or similar reactions.*

Once an old man sat beneath a busy bridge. He was soaking wet and all alone. (Was he happy or sad?) Beside him sat a torn paper bag, a broken stick, and a little dog.

A young boy happened by with a fishing pole in hand and spotted the old man. "Good morning," the boy shouted. The dog looked up, but the old man didn't move or answer. (Was he asleep [happy face] or angry [sad face]?) The boy wasn't sure. So he called out again, "Good morning, sir."

This time the old man carefully moved, sat up, and looked over at the young boy. (Did he have a happy face or a sad face?) He flashed a toothless smile at the boy and said, "I'm so glad you've come. I was riding my bicycle when a big truck sideswiped me, throwing me off my bike and into the water. The truck didn't stop! I'm wet and cold and believe I have a broken arm. Can you help me?" (Was the boy afraid or happy to help?)

The boy quickly answered, "I will help you." Then he turned, ran up the bank, and waved down a passing police car. The policeman came and carefully lifted the old man into his car and drove him to the hospital. (Was he glad to be at the hospital or sad?) Meanwhile the boy took the old man's dog home, dried him off, and fed him. (Was the dog happy to be fed or did it growl at the boy?) His mother thought it was a stray and would go away.

The next morning the boy's mother found this story in the newspaper and asked her son if he'd heard about it. He said he had, and told her the whole story. (Was she angry at her son?) "We must go to the hospital and see the old man to make sure he is still OK," she said. They went together, found the man who was by now feeling (give happy or sad sign). The old man thanked the boy for his help. Then the boy told the old man he had taken care of his dog, too (happy/sad sign). The old man was so (happy/sad sign) that he told the boy that the dog had just begun to follow him, but he had no way to take care of it. He asked the boy and his mother if they'd like to have the dog. (Were they happy or sad?) They were very happy to get the dog, and took care of him for many years. The old man was soon released from the hospital and went to see the family that had helped him in his emergency. He was again a (happy/sad) man, and so was the boy, his mother, and the little dog!

When you do kind things for others, how does it make you feel? (Happy or sad?)

When you do kind things for others, how does it make your mother or father feel? (Happy or sad?)

How do you think this made Satan feel? (Happy or angry?)

How do you think this made Jesus feel? (Happy or sad?)

You can read a similar story in Luke 10:30-37.

Meaningful Stories

71

He Could Only Whittle a Stick

Antonio loved music, but he couldn't sing a note. He wanted to sing like his friends but his voice was, well, squeaky. All he could do was listen to his friends sing and play, while he just whittled on a stick.

Once a year a big festival came to town, and it was the custom for children to go into the streets and sing or play their instruments. It was all part of the fun. Sometimes people would stop, listen, applaud, and perhaps even hand them a coin or two. So being musical was definitely an advantage. But that was not Antonio's gift. All he could do was to listen to his friends—and whittle on a stick.

One morning Antonio went to the festival to watch his friends get rich from those who paused to listen to them. One well-dressed man asked them to sing their song a second time. They were amazed, but did, and he dropped a gold piece into their hands! Then with a nod, he left. The boys were stunned. They looked at each other and said, "That was Amati! The GREAT Amati!"

"Who's Amati? And why do you call him 'great'?" Antonio asked. His friends just laughed at him and said to themselves, "How could he know? Antonio doesn't know anything about music. All he can do is listen and whittle on a stick." Then they told him that Amati and his family made fine violins, some of the best in all of Italy.

A violin maker? Antonio thought. *Aren't they made of wood? Does he carve them?* A thought stirred in his mind, and he determined to meet this great violin maker. *Maybe I can't sing, but someday I could whittle a violin, and it could make music.* The idea wouldn't leave him. He quickly made a little plan.

Early the next morning Antonio gathered some things he'd whittled and struck out to find Amati's house. Carefully he knocked and called, and eventually the great Amati himself came to the door. Quickly Antonio pulled things he'd carved from his pockets and stuttered "Aaare they any ggood? Could I make a violin?"

"Well, are you musical?" Amati asked.

"No," he responded sadly. "I can only whittle on a stick. But I like to listen to my friends sing, and play, and . . ."

"What is your name?" Amati asked.

"My name is Aaantonio Sstradivari, and I lllove mmmusic."

"Ah," the great Amati said, "There are many ways to make good music, but it's the song in your heart that really matters."

Antonio never forgot Amati's words, and eventually his dream came

84 Interactive Family Worship Ideas for Kids

true. The great Amati allowed him to work in his violin shop. At first he carved only decorative trim for Amati's fine instruments. But what he did was excellent. And each day he watched and learned the secrets Mr. Amati would teach him. Eventually, Antonio made his first violin, and proudly wrote on it: "Student of Nicol'o Amatai." And it wasn't long before he, too, became a violin maker. And an excellent one as well!

Today Antonio Stradivari is considered one of the greatest violin makers ever. He also made violoncellos and violas—all of them superbly made. Some of those instruments are in museums, and some are still being played in orchestras around the world . . . all of them made by the hands of a little boy who couldn't sing, but could only whittle on a stick—with excellence!

Solomon was a musician too. And everything he did was done well, because God gave him extraordinary skill and wisdom. He has been called the wisest man to ever live. And, like Antonio, he loved music and carried a song in his heart. With God's blessing you can become skilled at anything you wish as well, even if you start out . . . *just whittling on an old dry stick!*

Meaningful Stories

72 Amazing George

They said he was a useless little boy. But give some "useless" people even half a chance, and with God's help, they can amaze the world.

Many years ago a boy named George, along with his mother, was kidnapped by some scary men and sold as slaves. His mother disappeared, and George never saw her again. His father had been killed in a farm accident when he was just an infant. His owners, Moses and Susan Carver, then raised him.

As a very young child, George learned to appreciate nature. He loved plants and flowers, and spent much time outdoors. Because of his ability to help plants grow, he earned the nickname "the plant doctor." About the age of 12 (around the year 1877), he traveled to a nearby town to attend a school for Black children. He slept all winter in a cold barn, did odd jobs around town for meals, and went to school.

He worked hard and earned enough money to go to college. Although the school accepted him, when it found out he was Black it turned him away. But he was a good student and didn't give up, and eventually enrolled at another college.

After he completed his courses at a second college, that one invited him to serve as a teacher. It offered him a place to live and work at the very thing he loved most—studying plants. His research combined with his days of wandering in the fields as a boy made him an amazing scientist. He had a very bright mind and wanted to use his knowledge and skills to help people, especially Black people like himself.

He noticed that his people ate a lot of peanuts and sweet potatoes. They couldn't afford a cow, so their children seldom or never got milk. This bothered him. He experimented with peanuts in his plant laboratory and discovered that he could make from peanuts a "milk" rich in protein just like cow's milk. No one had ever heard of such a thing as peanut milk! But it was true, and his discovery helped many people get better nutrition.

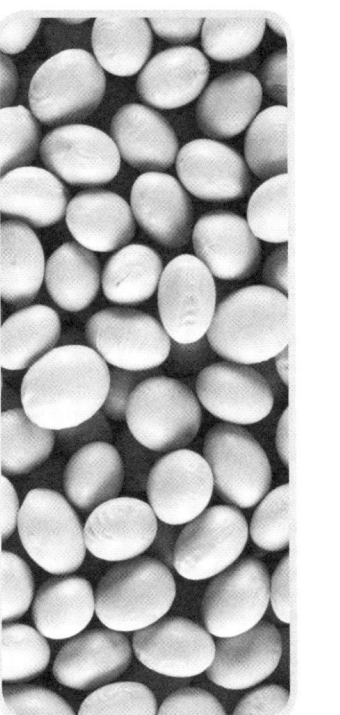

Farmers in the South had been planting cotton for many years, season after season. The cotton crops wore out the soil, however. So Carver encouraged the farmers to plant sweet potatoes, peanuts, and soybeans instead of cotton. They were easy to grow and would help restore the soil, he said. Because the farmers planted peanuts, they found themselves with a huge crop of peanuts but no market for them. Now they were mad at Carver. The story goes that he locked himself in his laboratory and asked God why He made the peanut. Later he developed more than 300 products that could be made from peanuts and the peanut plant—such things as glue, wood filler, axle grease, printer's ink, hand lotion, shoe polish, medicines, shampoo, laundry soap, and the list goes on and on.

The next time someone tells you that something is impossible, remember how God watched over George Washington Carver and showed him many things that are still benefiting us today. The Bible says: "A lazy man will soon be poor, but hard work will reward the diligent" (Proverbs 10:4, Clear Word). George Washington Carver was a very faithful and hardworking man whose work God blessed.

Meaningful Stories

Faithful to the End
The Story of John Nevins Andrews

John Nevins Andrews was born in 1829. His parents were poor and his early boyhood simple, but he was an excellent student and a hard worker. He would memorize Scripture as he plowed. John quit school at the age of 11 but had memorized the New Testament.

His uncle Charlie was a congressperson in Washington, D.C., and took note of John's keen mind. He badly wanted his nephew to become a senator and offered to pay his way to college. John said he'd think about it, but began preaching instead.

It was about this time that John and his parents heard the evangelist William Miller preach about the second coming of Christ. They believed Miller's studies were right and that Jesus would come, perhaps as early as 1844. They and many other families became "Millerites," followers of William Miller. But Jesus did not come in 1844. Many just gave up the whole idea. But John Andrews and few others continued studying the Bible and discovered other Bible truths. They found that the seventh day was God's Sabbath and began keeping it holy. John showed others the texts, and soon many were observing the Sabbath with him.

In 1856 he married Angeline Stevens. During the next few years Charles and Mary were born to the couple, and later two more children came along, but both of those died as babies. And then, just 16 years later, Angeline died. Pastor John and Mary and Charles were devastated. With Angeline gone John had no one to help with the care of his home or family, but the little family of three hung together and pressed forward in spite of the pain.

A few years later the budding Seventh-day Adventist Church wanted to send a missionary to Switzerland. John Andrews was their first choice. So in September of 1874 well-wishers waved the family goodbye as the three sailed out of Boston Harbor, making John Nevins Andrews the first official missionary sent overseas by the Seventh-day Adventist Church.

Life in a foreign land was difficult. After about a year the family's money began running low. They had spent most of it on printing. Mary decided to get a little job picking grapes to earn extra cash for buying groceries. It was hard work, but she determined to do all she could to help.

To learn the language faster, Mary, Charles, and their father decided they'd speak French all day, except between 5:00 and 6:00 in the evening, when they used English. During that time Mary and Charles talked fast so as to get as much said as possible!

But it didn't take long before the little missionary family got their life better organized. Mary would do the cooking, and Charles would buy the groceries. But when he went to the market, no one understood what he wanted—he couldn't speak to them, nor could they understand him, so he simply pointed to the fruit and vegetables he wanted, held up the money, and came home with an armload of food and a big smile.

Because she learned the French language so quickly, Mary was soon able to help her father by copyediting the French *Signs of the Times*. The family worked hard, and the endless work and long hours eventually took its toll on their health. Mary got sick. Very sick!

It was about this time that John Andrews received a letter from the church leaders in America requesting that he come to the General Conference session back in America to tell about the progress of his work in Switzerland. *Perfect,* he thought. *I'll take Mary, and we'll also see Dr. John Harvey Kellogg. Perhaps he can cure her.* Charles stayed in Switzerland and kept their work going.

But in America Dr. Kellogg had bad news. Mary had tuberculosis, and immediately he put her in the hospital. He said the disease was very contagious. In spite of his warnings her father stayed by her side day and night until she died. She was only 17. It was still another tragedy for the family, and John Andrews felt her loss deeply.

Eventually John returned to Switzerland and was thrilled to see Charles again, but soon John too became sick with tuberculosis! Still he continued to write while propped up in his bed. He died from tuberculosis at only 54 and was buried in Basel, Switzerland.

During his lifetime he had memorized much of the Bible and spoke seven different languages. He served as president of the General Conference, and much more. Truly he was God's faithful servant to the end.

Let's be faithful too, so that Jesus can say to us, as I'm sure He will to John Andrews, "Well done, faithful servant, enter into the joy of the Lord."

74 — I Was Blind, but Now I See!

There he was, sitting in the dirt along the side of the road. It was hot and dusty. People passed nearby, but he had a certain stench around him that repulsed them. The combined smell of dirt, body odor, urine, and animal waste that can accumulate on someone who cannot bathe and spends most of his time sitting on the ground kept people from stopping to chat or even come near. But he couldn't help it. Being blind, he was unable to find his way to a pool to bathe. The only things he could do were to listen and beg. Day after day, after day, after day.

This day had been no different than any other. Boring. Hot. Dusty. Little response for his persistent begging. He could hear people passing by, and children laughing and chasing each other. He could hear the sounds of donkey hooves and the slapping of leather thongs against bare feet. So he cried out to anyone who might hear, asking what the commotion was about. And someone answered: *Jesus of Nazareth is coming.*

Jesus? That name struck him like a thunderbolt. Having heard of Him and how He healed people, he immediately cried out, "Jesus, Son of David, please have mercy on me!" But some in the crowd quickly scolded him and told him to be quiet and stop shouting! That made him scream all the louder, "Son of David, have mercy on me!"

When He reached the place where the blind man sat, Jesus stopped, requested someone to bring the man to him, and then asked what he wanted? "Lord, I want to be able to see."

There was immediate silence and a pause that seemed to the blind man like an eternity. Jesus knew that sin had filled the man's life. But he was full of faith. With a big smile Jesus said to the man, "Your faith has brought you forgiveness, and I give you your sight as well!" The blind man looked in the direction of the words, and instantly his crusty eyes opened and he could see—clear and distinct for the first time in many years. He saw trees, and people, and animals, and . . . the smile on Jesus' face. It was a miracle!

As the crowd began to move again, the man walked close to Jesus and repeatedly thanked Him for the gift of sight and for forgiving him of his sins.

We can never thank Jesus enough for forgiving our sins, or for the gift of sight. Let's remember to walk close to Him every day.

Read this story in Luke 18:35-43.

Let the Music Begin!
Rewritten from *The Great Controversy*, pages 635-652

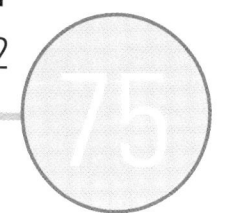

The book The Great Controversy *gives a sweeping look at the world and God's people just before and after Jesus comes the second time. Here is a brief glance at times yet to come, rewritten with a little artistic license, from pages 635-652.*

It's midnight. The world is fast coming to an end! Jesus is about to reveal His awesome power. The world is a mess! Everything in nature is out of control. The sun is shining bright even in the middle of the night! Streams stop flowing. Angry clouds form, and wicked people are terrified by all the crazy things they see and hear around them.

Then, through the middle of the angry clouds, comes a blast of brilliant light, and out of it the sound of God's voice saying: *"It is done."* His words shake the earth with a powerful earthquake. Whole mountains roll and shake like straw in the wind, and huge boulders are thrown from their tops. Strange screams are heard as though from the winds of a hurricane. The ocean rolls like a sheet in the wind. Lightning blasts the earth and sets it on fire. Wicked people are terrified. Even the devil trembles before God's power. Suddenly graves are thrown open and millions of people rise to see Jesus appear in all His glory.

Through a break in the clouds there appears a white star. Those who have not obeyed God see it as an indication of His anger, but it promises hope to God's faithful people. His people remember the words written by David: *"God is our refuge and strength, a very present help in trouble. Therefore will not we fear, though the earth be removed, and though the mountains be carried into the midst of the sea. . . . The Lord of hosts is with us; the God of Jacob is our refuge"* (Psalm 46:1-7). Soon the scary dark clouds disappear, revealing the awesome city of God. Then a hand appears in the sky holding two stones folded together. They are opened, and all humanity sees God's Ten Commandments. Everyone around the whole world reads these words in their own language. Millions admit they have no excuse for not keeping God's laws, and they hear God say to them: *"Depart, thou wicked servant."*

But God's faithful people throughout the world, and from all ages past, are caught up and begin to fly through the air to meet Jesus—their journey to heaven begins.

Meaningful Stories

Fast-forward! With unimaginable joy, Jesus welcomes His faithful people to their heavenly home. They gather at the sea of glass and watch Jesus meet Adam and Eve. This is the first time they've done so since being separated at the Garden of Eden. Jesus hugs them both again. And even though Jesus had to die for their sins, He forgives them for the wrong they did. God's people who look on are thrilled and break into singing. It's a song which only they know, because no one else in the universe has ever lived in a world of sin like them. No one else understands what it's like to feel guilty for sin. But those memories are gone. Now they're with Jesus. *Let the music begin!* Let the new sights and sounds, the new colors, the expanded minds, the space travel, the family reunions, all begin! Higher than anyone's highest imagination are God's plans for His people. They will now live with boundless energy in a perfect world, forever!

The Lisbon Earthquake
Rewritten from *The Great Controversy,* pages 304, 305

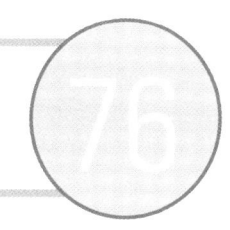

It was 1755. Was the world about to end?

One day Jesus and His disciples gathered on top of the Mount of Olives, and Jesus began telling them of things that would happen in the future. One of them asked, "What will be the sign that [these things] are about to take place?" (Luke 21:7, NIV) Jesus answered, "There will be great earthquakes, famines, and pestilences in various places" (verse 11, NIV). And exactly as Jesus prophesied, it happened. What God says always comes true. His Word never fails.

In 1755 a terrible earthquake shook Lisbon, Portugal. It extended as well into most of Europe, Africa, and even into America. People also felt it in Greenland, the West Indies, Norway, Sweden, Great Britain, and Ireland. In a village near Morocco it completely swallowed up 8,000 to 10,000 people. The quake created a wave so large that it swept over the coast of Spain and Africa, wiping out whole cities and creating terrible destruction as it went. In one city (Cadiz) the wave was said to be 60 feet high.

In Lisbon a violent shock threw down the greater part of the city, and in six minutes 60,000 people perished. A great number had gathered on a huge marble wharf where boats came to dock, thinking it to be a safe place, but suddenly the entire wharf sank with all the people on it, and not one of the bodies ever floated to the surface.

The quake caused churches, large public buildings, and more than one fourth of the homes in the city to collapse. Fires broke out and raged with violence for almost three days, leaving the city of Lisbon decimated. Those who still lived ran here and there in confusion and terror, beating themselves and screaming, "The world's at an end!" Some have estimated that 90,000 people died that terrible day.

Jesus had said long years before that "there will be great earthquakes," and there was!

Activity: See who can stack the tallest tower of Cheerios before the tower collapses. You have 60 seconds. Now try it with mini shredded wheat.

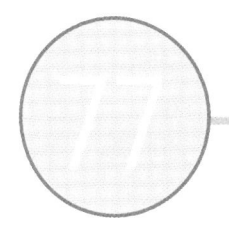

Darkening of the Sun, and the Moon Turns Red

Rewritten from *The Great Controversy*, pages 306-308

Through the prophet Joel Jesus left a sign of the end of the world that would take place before He returns to earth: *"The sun shall be turned into darkness, and the moon into blood" (Joel 2:31)*. And 25 years after the Lisbon earthquake, Joel's prophetic words came true. Here's what happened:

On May 19, 1780, a mysterious darkening of the sun took place in New England. The morning sun rose full and bright as always, but soon there appeared a mysterious dark cloud. Lightning flashed, thunder rolled, and a bit of rain fell. By 9:00 the clouds took on a strange coppery color, then a heavy black cloud quickly spread over the entire area, and it became as dark as it normally would be at 9:00 in the evening. Men came in from working in the fields, others closed their shops, school was let out, and children fled home in terror. Chickens returned to their roosts, cows ambled in from the fields, and even frogs began their evening peeping. By 11:00 in the morning the darkness was at its worst. People could not see anything except by candlelight. No one had ever seen anything like this before. It was frightening and seemed supernatural.

People gathered by candlelight in their churches, and everyone was asking, "What's happening? Is this the end of the world?" The pastors believed the strange event might be what had been prophesied about the end of the world.

The mysterious darkness spread across much of the northeastern United States as far north as the American settlements extended, west to the state of New York, and down the eastern coastline.

Just before sunset the sun appeared again, but it was only partially visible, hidden by a black heavy mist. Just after sunset the dark clouds returned, and the night grew dark very quickly. Even candlelight could barely be seen by nearby neighbors. The full moon shed very little light. About midnight the heavy darkness disappeared, and the moon took on the appearance of blood!

Hundreds of years before it happened, the prophet Joel predicted this strange event would take place, and now his words had come true: "The sun shall be turned into darkness, and the moon into blood" (Joel 2:31).

Jesus' words never fail, because He knows the future and reveals it to His prophets. We can count on their words, because they write only what God shows them will be. They will not fail!

Activity: Draw a red circle on a piece of paper. Stare at it for 15 seconds under a bright light. Now quickly close your eyes tight. Do you see the dark moon?

John Wycliffe
Rewritten from *The Great Controversy,* pages 79-96

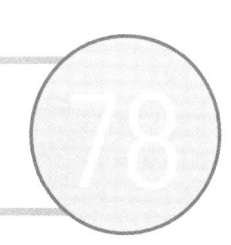

A long, long, time ago, even before your great-great-grandparents were born, evil men had charge of many of the churches in Europe. Dressing in richly colored robes, they looked and acted very important. Although they claimed to speak for God in church matters, they were more interested in getting money than helping the poor learn about God. They forced the common people to worship the way they said. So poor people, rich people, and even kings would obey whatever they said, because the priests claimed that God would be angry if they didn't and would throw them into a burning pit of fire that would torture them forever! (Does that sound like a God of love?)

They also told the people that only the educated priests, such as themselves, could understand the Bible, claiming that it was much too difficult for simple people like them. The priests made up other rules, such as, "If you pay me enough money, I will give you a piece of paper that says all your sins will be forgiven" (can any human being forgive our sins?) or "If you pay the church enough money, you and all your relatives and friends can go straight to heaven when you die. But if you don't, remember how hot that burning pit can get, 'cause you'll soon be in it!" (Could you love a God who would treat you like that?) And so the people obeyed the priests out of fear of going to the hot place. By this method the priests made lots of money for the church. And God saw it all.

The church tried to control who could read the Bible. Satan knew that if people could have Bibles, they would learn that God loved and cared for them and that all these rules were not from God, but evil human beings.

But God would not allow His Word to be snuffed out. As a young university student named John Wycliffe studied the Bible, he discovered truths that he'd never heard before. And he just couldn't keep them to himself. He shared the things he learned with his friends.

When the priests heard that Wycliffe was gaining an influence greater than their own, it filled the papal leaders with rage. But the more clearly Wycliffe understood the errors of the priests, the more earnestly he presented the truths from God's Word.

Suddenly his work came to a halt. Satan attacked him with a terrible sickness. The priests were thrilled. They thought he would finally repent of the "evil" he'd done to their church. They hurried to his side to listen to his confession. Representatives from various religious groups gathered around the supposedly dying man and said, "You have death on your lips. Repent of your evil ways and take back the things you've said against us." After listening patiently, he then asked someone to raise him up in his bed. He looked at all of them and said in a strong voice that made them tremble: "I shall not die, but live; and again expose your evil deeds." Astonished and embarrassed, the men hurried from his room. He did live and said many more things against these men and their evil system.

John Wycliffe was truly a man used by God. In reading the Bible, he found that Jesus was the only one who stands for all people everywhere. He gave himself to the service of Christ and determined to proclaim the truths he had discovered. And he changed the life of millions by translating the old ancient Bible into English so that all could read it for themselves. It was called the greatest work of his lifetime. He also had Bibles copied in English, which soon found their way into the homes of many.

It was the beginning of a time of change called "the Reformation." The church was losing its grip, its rules and requirements were disgusting people. And John Wycliffe was the first of many Reformers to follow, which is why he has been called "the Morning Star of the Reformation." Like the early-morning star that shines brightly in the east, John Wycliffe shone in God's eyes brighter than all others of his time. He showed the people, rich and poor, God's true system through God's Word, then opened the way for many other Reformers to do the same. And God saw it all—*and was pleased!*

79 Stand Tall

Instructions: *Show your answer to these questions by standing if you agree, or remain seated if you disagree.*

1. If you think John Wycliffe learned a new language to read the old Bible, stand tall.
2. If you think John Wycliffe was amazed at the new things he read in the old Bible, stand tall.
3. If you think John Wycliffe obeyed his church's teachings after reading the Bible, stand tall.
4. If you think John Wycliffe didn't tell anyone what he found in the Bible, stand tall.
5. If you think John Wycliffe had heard these Bible teachings many times before, stand tall.
6. If you think Satan was happy with John Wycliffe for discovering these Bible truths, stand tall.
7. If you think the church leaders were pleased with John Wycliffe, stand tall.
8. If you think John Wycliffe believed he was going to die from sickness, stand tall.
9. If you think John Wycliffe's greatest accomplishment was being a good student, stand tall.
10. If you think John Wycliffe had Bibles copied in the English language, stand tall.
11. If you think John Wycliffe was called the "roaring wonder of the Reformation," stand tall.
12. If you think John Wycliffe was the only Reformer God ever had, stand tall.
13. If you think God used John Wycliffe to spread good things about God, stand tall.

Ulrich Zwingli [God's Swiss Reformer]
Based on *The Great Controversy*, pages 171-184

God does not always choose men or women who are important, rich, or powerful to do His work. *It is often His plan to select humble, simple people and through them accomplish great things. Ulrich Zwingli was a good example of this.*

He was born in the home of a humble herder who lived in the beautiful Alps of Switzerland. These mountains were the perfect environment to train his bright mind about the greatness and power of God. And his godly grandmother taught him about the great men and women of the Bible.

Zwingli could play several instruments, including the violin, harp, flute, dulcimer, and hunting horn. He would sometimes amuse children with his lute. He wrote several hymns published in some hymnals of the time.

Zwingli's father wanted him to have a good education. His son's mind was sharp and developed quickly, which made it difficult to find teachers for him in his valley home. At the early age of 13 he went to the most distinguished school in Switzerland. But here a danger arose that threatened his future. The Dominican religious order tried to entice him to enter a convent. They saw that his youthfulness and natural ability as a speaker and writer as well as his genius for music and poetry would bring money to them. But his father found out about their intentions and told him to come home immediately. Although he obeyed, he could not be happy in his little valley for long and moved to Basel. It was here that Zwingli first heard that God's grace was free—a new thought to him. He said that "it was like the early-morning light that comes before dawn."

Eventually he was ordained to the priesthood and proved to be a good pastor. The more he studied the Scriptures the more he saw the contrast between what God said in His Word and what his church was teaching. He continued studying and praying, asking the Holy Spirit to help him understand.

In 1516 Zwingli was invited to become a preacher in Einsiedeln, far from his home in the Alps. Among the chief attractions there was a statue of Mary that supposedly could work miracles. Every year people came from all over Switzerland, France, and Germany to see the statue. On one occasion Zwingli took pity on the people and told them that they could have liberty only through Jesus. "Don't imagine," he said, "that God is in this temple more than any other part of creation. Wherever you come from, God is around you, and hears you." To many it was a new thought. Some didn't believe it.

But another group gladly accepted the tidings of righteousness through Christ. They returned to their homes and told others what they had learned, and so the truth spread from town to town and village to village. In time the shrine of Mary drew less and less attention and the offerings dropped off. And even though his salary fell as well, Zwingli was pleased to know that the power of superstitious belief in the image of Mary was being broken and people were believing in the Bible.

Interest in what he taught led people of all classes to come to his church in great numbers to listen to his preaching. He opened the Gospels and taught the people about the life, teachings, and death of Christ. "It is to Christ that I desire to lead you—to Christ, the true source of salvation."

In 1519 a serious plague swept over Switzerland. It caused men and women seriously to consider their eternal life, and they longed for a more solid understanding of truth than the church was offering them. The disease struck Zwingli himself, and a rumor circulated that he was dead. When he got well he began to preach with even greater fervor. Zwingli had arrived at a clearer understanding of the truth and had personally experienced its renewing power. The people felt the value of the gospel as never before, and the local cathedral filled to overflowing with crowds that came to hear him speak.

Step by step the Reformation advanced. Alarmed, Zwingli's enemies made repeated attacks against him. Not only did they kill some of those who followed his teachings, they wanted him dead as well. Zwingli, who had been preaching the gospel for four years in Zurich, said, "It was more quiet and peaceful than any other town; is not, then, Christianity the best safeguard of the general security?" His opponents couldn't disagree.

But they decided to have a debate with Zwingli. They would choose the place and the judges who would decide who the winner was. Though Zwingli was not present, his presence was felt. He received a daily account of what was said through a student who made a faithful record each day. Two other students delivered them to Zwingli, who wrote his response at night, and the students returned them to Baden the next morning. He was thus able to take part, though from a distance.

The debate lasted 18 days. At its close Zwingli's opponents claimed victory, but not long afterward the cities of Bern and Basel declared for the Reformation. The people wanted change. Did God's cause win? Yes, as it always will.

If you were Satan, what kind of miracle would you have the statue of Mary do to fool people into believing it was God's doing?

What does God say in His Word about making or worshipping idols? (See Exodus 20:4; 1 Corinthians 10:19, 20; Exodus 34:17.)

Does the Bible tell anywhere of a statue (idol) performing a miracle? (No. The Bible is full of miracle stories, but none of them have to do with an idol doing anything.)

Prayer and Praise Ideas

Here are some creative prayer and voice choir ideas to use with family worship.

6

81 Prayer Variations
Praise by Categories

Instructions: *Explain to the family that you are inviting them to join in the worship prayer. And when you name a category to be thankful for, and pause, the family will fill in the specifics. Example: If Father says food, someone might say bread, another peaches, watermelon, or spaghetti, etc., around the circle. When all have had a turn, close the prayer.*

The prayers might include several categories from this list:

- **people**
- **flowers**
- **Sabbath**
- **sky**
- **food**
- **colors**
- **missionaries**
- **animals**

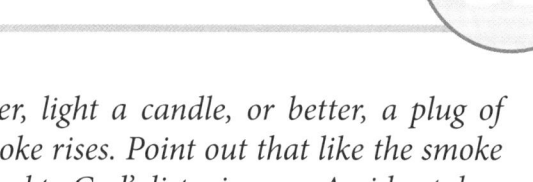

82 Prayer Smoke

Instructions: *Before the evening prayer, light a candle, or better, a plug of incense, and let the kids watch as the smoke rises. Point out that like the smoke rising upward, so too do our prayers ascend to God's listening ear. An idea taken from David's prayer: "Let my prayer be set before You as incense, the lifting up of my hands as the evening sacrifice" (Psalm 141:2, NKJV). Discuss this concept.*

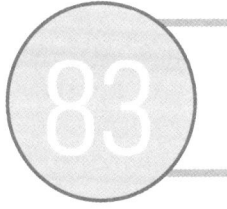

83 Prayer Diversity

Instructions: *It's always rewarding to hear men and women pray. But it means even more when children are included. When there's a group, try asking several to pray, including, perhaps, one adult woman, a teen boy, a girl 10 or under, and/or an adult male. Each of these prayers should be short. You will enjoy the diversity even more if someone prays in another language.*

Interactive Family Worship Ideas for Kids

Five-Finger Prayer

84

The thumb is nearest to you. So begin by praying for those closest to you.

The index finger is your pointing finger. Pray for those who teach and instruct, including teachers, doctors, and ministers.

The middle finger is the tallest finger. Pray for our president, leaders, and administrators.

The ring finger is our weakest finger. Pray for those who are weak, in trouble, or in pain.

The little finger is the smallest finger. See yourself as the least of all, so pray for yourself.

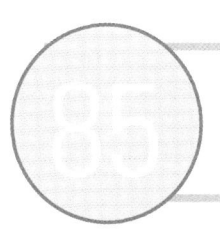

85

The Lord's Prayer

Don't forget to repeat the Lord's Prayer together. Our family used to say it every Friday night.

Pay Up!

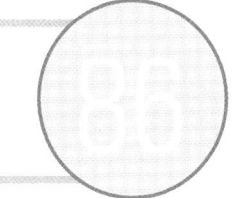

86

Here is a parable that Jesus told that will come to life with group participation. Photocopy the page, choose a reader, a king, and a poor servant, and let everyone else participate as shown. The parable appears in Matthew 18:23-35.

The parable of a forgiving king and a less-than-forgiving servant!

Reader 1: The kingdom of heaven is like a king who wanted to settle his accounts with his servants. A man who owed him several million dollars was brought to him. Here's the story:

King: I need the several million dollars you owe me! Pay up now!

Everyone: Uh, I can't pay.

King *(demanding voice)*: Pay up!

Prayer and Praise Ideas   101

Everyone: I can't pay.

King *(demanding voice):* Sell his wife!

Everyone *(begging voice):* Please don't.

King *(demanding voice):* Sell him or throw him in jail!

Everyone *(begging voice):* Please don't!

King *(demanding voice):* Sell his children and his land as well!

Everyone *(whimpering voice):* Please, please don't!

Reader: The servant fell on his knees and cried:

Everyone *(begging voice):* Please, please be patient with me.

Reader: And so the king kindly took pity on him.

King: I will cancel his debt. Let him go free. Don't sell his estate.

Everyone *(excited voice):* I am free! I am free! I'm freeeeee!

Reader: But then the servant went out and found one of his fellow servants who owed him just a few dollars and demanded payment from him.

Everyone *(demanding voice):* Pay up!

Poor servant: I can't pay.

Everyone *(demanding voice):* Pay up!

Poor servant: I can't pay.

Everyone *(demanding voice):* Sell his wife!

Poor servant *(whimpering voice):* Please don't sell my wife.

Everyone *(demanding voice):* Sell him or throw him in jail!

Poor servant *(whimpering voice):* Please, please, don't!

Everyone *(demanding voice):* Sell his children and his land!

Poor servant *(whimpering voice):* Please don't sell my family. I'll pay soon.

Reader: So the servant's servant fell on his knees and cried:

Poor servant *(begging voice):* Please, be patient. I will pay as soon as I can.

Everyone *(demanding voice):* Sell him!

King: I forgave you millions of dollars because you pleaded with me. Can't you forgive your debtors the few dollars they owe you as well?

Reader: And so it was that Jesus showed us what true forgiveness means. We must forgive others just as we want them to forgive us.

When the Debate Ends

87

Instructions: *Here is a responsive reading inspired by the last four paragraphs of* The Great Controversy *(pp. 677, 678), with modifications for clarity for young minds. Father, young boys, young girls, Mother, and everyone will read as shown. Read it with anticipation.*

FATHER: When the great controversy with Satan and sin has ended,

BOYS: sin will be no more.

EVERYONE: The entire universe will be clean again.

GIRLS: Harmony and gladness will beat throughout everything God has made.

BOYS: From God will flow life and light, and everything, everywhere will be happy.

MOTHER: From the tiniest speck to the greatest worlds in space, all things will be perfect.

EVERYONE: All beings, and all things in their own way, will say, *God is love.*

FATHER: And as the years of eternity roll by we will understand more and more about our awesome God and His amazing Son, Jesus.

MOTHER: Our love and happiness, and our knowledge of God, will increase with the years.

EVERYONE: And as Jesus tells us about the incredible story of redemption and how He overcame Satan, we will be totally amazed at this awesome story of endless love.

FATHER: All the secrets of the universe will be open for us to study.

MOTHER: We will be able to fly to far distant worlds without getting tired.

BOYS:	We will meet beings from distant planets who have watched us struggle,
MOTHER:	and thrilled when we took our stand against sin and for Jesus.
EVERYONE:	We will talk with them, and they will teach us things they have learned about God's amazing creation.
FATHER:	We will join them and marvel as we see suns, and stars, and complete heavenly systems circle around God's throne.
EVERYONE:	Upon everything, from the least to the greatest, God's name is stamped and His power is seen.
FATHER:	And near the end of the Bible, John, the writer of Revelation, says: "And every creature which is in heaven and on the earth and under the earth and such as are in the sea, and all that are in them, I heard saying,
MOTHER:	Blessing
GIRLS:	and honor
BOYS:	and glory and power
EVERYONE:	be to them who sits on the throne, and to the Lamb, forever and ever!" (Revelation 5:13, NKJV).

Voices for the Sabbath
A Voice Choir for Sundown Worship

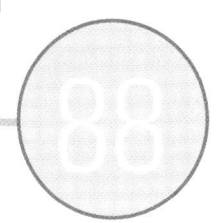

Instructions: *Give everyone a copy of the text below, appoint voices 1 and 2, and let everyone participate.*

ALL:	Remember the Sabbath day to keep it holy.
VOICE 1:	Because this was the day God ceased His work of creating.
ALL:	For in six days the Lord made the heavens and the earth,
CHILDREN:	the sea,
VOICE 2:	and all that is within them—visible and invisible,
MEN:	whether thrones or dominions,
WOMEN:	or principalities,
CHILDREN:	or powers.
ALL:	All things were created through Him and for Him.
PAUSE:	
VOICE 2:	Then God rested from all His work, blessed the Sabbath day, and declared it holy.
MEN:	So in six days we too, should labor, and do all of our work.
WOMEN:	But on the Sabbath day we rest, our sons and our daughters,
MEN:	our male and female servants,
CHILDREN:	even the cattle, and special friends who might be with us.
WOMEN:	Because we rest we enjoy the Sabbath even more, and speak of it with delight, a special day which the Lord Himself set aside for us.
VOICE 2:	So let us honor the Lord through what we say and do today . . .
VOICE 1:	Then the Lord promises He will be our delight . . .
ALL:	For the mouth of the Lord has spoken it, and His fingers have sealed these words in stone. Amen.

[Based on Exodus 20; Isaiah 58; Genesis 2; and Colossians 1.]

Prayer and Praise Ideas   105

The Twenty-third Psalm
Say It With Ribbons

Instructions: *Cut out strands of **white, green, blue, brown, black, yellow, red,** and **gold** ribbon, approximately six to eight inches long, and give one strand to each person. Read the psalm together using a familiar version of Scripture, then repeat it as you pin the colors together. Say it again using the colored ribbon as a key to each phrase.*

Gold:
"The Lord is my shepherd; I shall not want.

Green:
"He makes me lie down in green pastures;

Blue:
"He leads me beside the still waters. He restores my soul.

Brown:
"He leads me in the paths of righteousness for His name's sake;

Black:
"Yea, though I walk through the valley of the shadow of death, I will fear no evil; for You are with me;

Yellow:
"Your rod and Your staff, they comfort me.

Red:
"You prepare a table before me in the presence of my enemies; You anoint my head with oil; my cup runs over.

White:
"Surely goodness and mercy shall follow me all the days of my life; and I shall dwell in the house of the Lord forever" (NKJV).

"Popcorn" Prayer

Instructions: *"Popcorn" prayer is a fun approach that allows many people to participate. Such prayers begin with a short "introduction" by the "leader," who then pauses, allowing others to join in as they wish. Anyone can jump in with a short prayer thought, praise, or a request. There is no particular order. Subject matter is optional or could be discussed before you begin. The leader who began will end the prayer.*

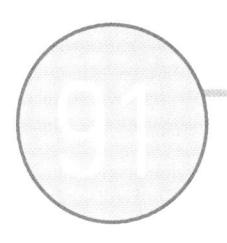

Pray 'n' Sing

Instructions: *Stand in a circle and hold hands. One might lead out, or use the popcorn prayer approach. Close by all singing "Thank You, Lord," and while holding hands, raise them together at the words "Thy great salvation so rich and free."*

So Much for Which to Be Thankful

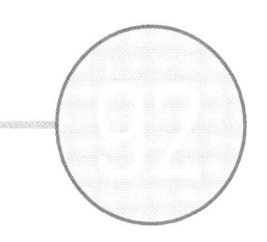

Instructions: *Sometime during the week, have the kids cut from magazines pictures of various fruits, vegetables, sunsets, pets, etc. Tape or glue each onto a toothpick, then stick each one in an orange or apple and use as a centerpiece for the table. At the evening mealtime, draw them out one at a time and each person will say what they are thankful for.*

Prayer and Praise Ideas

93. Praise Pretzels

Instructions: *I found this in an old church bulletin insert and couldn't resist including it here. Have the kids make "praise pretzels" by shaping the dough into letters that will form a phrase such as "Praise God" or "Happy Sabbath." At suppertime, have each person take a pretzel letter and tell something to praise God for that begins with that letter. For example: for the letter P one might say "peanuts," or "ponies," or "petunias," then ceremoniously eat the letter! This should make supper a "praise the Lord" event the kids will long remember.*

Pretzel recipe:

½ tablespoon yeast　　12 tablespoons sugar
¾ cup water　　2 cups flour
½ tablespoon salt　　1 beaten egg for glaze (optional)

Mix yeast, water, salt, and sugar. Gradually mix in flour and knead dough 3-4 minutes. Roll into long snakelike pieces according to the number of letters needed. Form the letters desired on a cookie sheet. Brush the letters with the egg and sprinkle additional salt (optional). Bake at 425°F for 15 minutes.

94. Colorful Prayers

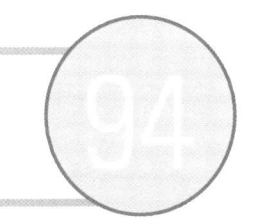

Instructions: *Photocopy, cut apart, and place prayers in a basket and invite each person to take one. One person starts, then each person prays specifically for their category.*

Praise for God's **POWER IN NATURE**
Thankful for **A SPECIFIC FOOD OR COLOR**
Pray for **A RELATIVE OR FRIEND.**
Our **PRESIDENT** and the leaders of our country
Thankful for **SAFETY THROUGH THE WEEK**
Pray for **THE MISSIONARIES** around the world.
Pray for the **LITERATURE EVANGELISTS AROUND THE WORLD.**
Pray for **SOMEONE WHO IS SICK.**
THE PASTORS and **LEADERS** of our denomination

A Baptismal Rite of Passage

Richmond, Virginia, June 14, 2013
When our oldest grandson was baptized, this is what we did to make it a special Friday evening worship experience.

Our two families and all the siblings gathered in a large circle in the living room. Each adult shared from his or her experience of baptism—when; where; who; how old; and unique memories, as well as personal feelings of being brought up out of the water. We thus affirmed Zachery in his decision to be baptized (and it happened that we drew out promises from the younger ones that they too wanted to follow Zachery's lead in baptism when they were old enough). We assured Zachery that it was the best decision he would ever make and was one of the three most important decisions he'd ever have to make in his lifetime, including graduation and marriage.

Then I demonstrated the process visually with a dirty old penny. I asked one of the brothers to pick out the dirtiest of five pennies, which I then soaked briefly in a clear glass of vinegar and three teaspoons of salt. It cleaned away the dirt perfectly, and I pulled out a bright, shiny penny. Then I pointed out that similarly a cleansing was happening to Zach's record of sins in heaven—now fresh and clean again—with his baptism.

We believe this worship affirmed and calmed his young mind and made his baptism the next day by his uncle Brennon easier and more meaningful.

It was a wonderful experience for everyone to review their own baptism again, and it was a worship that none of us will forget, especially Zachery.

We closed with a dedicatory prayer—*and a celebration!*